"SKIPPER" JACK

The story of an east coast beachman,
lifeboatman and fisherman.

Colin Tooke

A 'Norfolk' biography

© 1988 Colin Tooke and Poppyland Publishing
First published 1988
ISBN: 0 946148 33 3
Typesetting: PTPS
Cover Design: Top Floor Design
Cover Photography: Paul Damen
Printed by Printing Services (Norwich) Ltd.

Contents

Introduction	5
The Beachmen	7
"Skipjack"	15
Family Background	23
Lifeboats	33
The Mechanic	41
The Beachcomber	51
The Fisherman	59
A Volunteer	69

Lifeboatman, Fisherman, Beachman, John "Skipper" Woodhouse, a true sea-salt of the East Anglian coastline.(Paul Durrant)

INTRODUCTION

Beachman, fisherman, lifeboatman and historian, Freeman of the Borough of Great Yarmouth, and television personality. A collection of titles which at first glance appear to be an unusual mixture, but which go together - as the following chapters will show - when applied to one man, now in his seventies, who has lived and worked within sight and sound of the sea all his life.

There are few people left today who are true beachmen. But John Joseph Woodhouse of Caister-on-Sea, known to most as "Skipper," is a beachman through and through.

The inspiration to write this book came from many evenings listening to the tales and recollections of "Skipper" Woodhouse in the living room of his small cottage close to the Caister beach. On any dark winter evening the warmth of the fire draws in a continuous stream of people to talk about the day's fishing, the prospects for the morrow, or to recall events of yesteryear. As people come and go during the evening the topic of conversation is ever changing, and it was from these unique gatherings that much of the information for this book was obtained.

My thanks are due to the people whose conversations I have interrupted over the months, and who have tolerated my questions and given me much advice and encouragement. There are too many to name individually, but those in question will know who I mean.

"Skipper" and his brother, David, have been the main source of information for this book; and I must also thank their sister, Rose, who was able to fill in some of gaps; and Paul Durrant, for his constructive comments on fishing.

Unless otherwise stated the illustrations are taken from my own collection, and I thank Geoff Taylor for drawing the family tree. Today, Caister has the only voluntarily run full-size lifeboat in the country and "Skipper," although past the age when most men have retired, still takes an active interest. Indeed, one could say a very active interest. His experienced views are respected by the other members of the Caister Volunteer Rescue Service. He is also well known among lifeboatmen around the British coastline, and has friends in almost every seaside town or village which operates a lifeboat. He can also count among his friends many from across the sea, particularly the Dutch salvage crews with whom he has worked and co-operated on many occasions.

The book has also turned into a brief history of the Caister lifeboat service, but the events recorded here all have a link with "Skipper." It has also been necessary to trace back to the Haylett family to find the family roots. From the old books and documents which have survived from the early days of the Caister beach company I have been able to piece together the first chapters of this book.

"Skipper" is the present day custodian of many of these old records, and it has been with his help that a true picture has emerged of the days gone by, combining his memories of tales told when he was a boy with the now faded and yellowing books; books he has found so useful in the past, when numerous enquiries have been directed to him from far and wide.

Where I have allowed "Skipper's" own words to tell an incident, or portray his views, I have not tried to write in Norfolk dialect. No words could substitute for the real thing. The reader will have to imagine the rich drawl of a true Norfolk person.

The weather has always played an important part in the life of any beachman. If he is fishing or pleasure-tripping a sudden change in the weather can alter plans for the remainder of the day, and the following days. As a lifeboatman the bad weather of the winter months can mean a sudden call to duty to go to the aid of others. I have therefore headed each chapter of the book with a selection of "weather rhymes" to remind the reader of the importance of this natural element over which man has no control, but which can at times control man to an unprecedented degree.

The sand and sea have long since swallowed the footprints of the famous forebears of the Woodhouse family, but the elements have done nothing to erode their ancestral traditions.

When "Skipper" climbed aboard the Caister lifeboat *Charles Burton*, way back in 1933, he joined not only his father but also his grandfather in the crew. The following pages will unfold more of this story.

Colin Tooke
22 Beach Road
Caister-on-Sea

1988

THE BEACHMEN

When the sun goes down as clear as a bell
An easterly wind as sure as hell.

Many interesting and notable characters have emerged from among the seafaring communities of the East Anglian coastline during the past 200 years. Some have received national recognition and rewards for their work, but the majority have gone steadily about their daily business unnoticed and unrecorded. All have been beachmen and fishermen, many having been associated with the lifeboats stationed on these beaches, ready to go at a moment's notice and whatever the weather, to the aid of any seafarer in distress. These quiet, unassuming men have not sought recognition or reward for their work, seeing it as their duty to others.

The village of Caister, three miles north of the town of Great Yarmouth, has had a lifeboat station since 1845 and a beach company since the late 18th century. One of the most famous names from those early years was that of James "Jimmy" Haylett, the man who immortalized local beachmen with the words, "Caister men never turn back," a saying derived from a statement he made at an inquest into a lifeboat tragedy at the begining of the century.

The Hayletts were a predominant family in beach company circles, not only in Caister but in many villages to the north. And it is a descendant of this "Jimmy" Haylett who is the main character in this book, a story of a man who has lived and worked within sight of the sea all his life. A life given to fishing, salvage or any other gainful activity the coastline could provide to make a living, coupled with the less financially rewarding but necessary work of life saving, an activity where devotion to duty is essential and the rewards usually only those of satisfaction in knowing that you have done your best to help someone in trouble.

John Woodhouse, or "Skipper Jack" as he is better known locally, lives today with his brother, David, in a cottage close to his birthplace. It looks out over the sand dunes, with the lifeboat shed in the background, a scene that brings back constant reminders and tales of events both serious and amusing that have happened to him during the past seven decades. As a recognised historian of former lifeboat days he has been, and still is, the source for many researchers seeking information and advice. Today he is a popular guest speaker at many functions where his reminiscences of lifeboat services, recalled in great detail and sometimes with a wry sense of humour, keep his audiences enthralled throughout the evening.

Before inquiring into the life of "Skipper" Woodhouse it is necessary to look back into the history of lifeboats and beach companies

Caister beachmen c1880 outside their lookout and beach headquarters. The telescopes seen in this picture are still in use by the Volunteer Rescue Service over one hundred years later.(Ken Jary)

to understand why salvage work and lifesaving played such an important part in the lives of many people along this coastline throughout the 19th and well into the 20th century.

In a recently published book beachmen have been described as: "essentially a nautical Jack of all trades, turning their hand to anything which might offer a reward for their efforts. Much of their work was speculative, requiring a hunter's instinct and a good deal of personal effort to achieve a worthwhile result. Often enough it was extremely dull and arduous, providing little recompense for the patience and determination which was needed."

It is hard to think of a more suitable choice of words; and this description is appropriate to the subject of this book, a person who confesses he has never learnt to swim, has never had a need to swim, and although involved with countless rescues of other people, has been fortunate enough not to have been involved in any incident where he himself needed rescuing.

Caister is geographically placed on one of the most treacherous stretches of coastline in the British Isles. It has been calculated that, in the 19th century, over 50 per cent of all shipwrecks around Britain happened off the East Anglian coast. In the days of sailing traders this graveyard claimed countless lives and vessels during the periods of the winter gales. Bad navigation, ill equipped and poorly maintained vessels, together with the many sandbanks and shallow channels, proved too much for many seafarers. Incompetent officers with little or no knowledge of navigation, and captains prepared to risk the lives of their crews in order to get their ships to port on time, added to the dangers, and although any seaman could refuse to sail in any ship he considered unseaworthy the risk of ending up in jail was enough to deter most of them from complaining too much.

The record books are full of instances such as the night of November 1, 1789, when after a severe gale it was reported that 80 fishing vessels were wrecked and 120 bodies washed ashore between Yarmouth and Cromer.

A few years earlier, in 1781, when Armstrong was compiling his "History of Norfolk," he wrote: "Though Yarmouth Roads are very safe and the chief rendezvous of the colliers between Newcastle and London, and of other merchantmen, which are constantly passing and repassing, still the coast is particularly noted for being one of the most dangerous and most fatal to sailors in Britain, a melancholy instance of which happened about the year 1692 when above 200 sail of ships and above one thousand persons were lost in one night."

This observation was made at a time when the mariner had to look after himself. His fellow men on land had turned their backs to the sea, concentrating on agriculture for their daily needs. By the turn of the

The boats and equipment of the Caister beach company c1900. In front of the two lifeboats, 'Covent Garden' and 'Beauchamp', is the company gig 'Eclat'.

Lifeboat work in the nineteenth century was hard and dangerous. In this engraving the lifeboat attempts to get alongside the steamer 'Ontario', aground on Scroby Sands in October 1864.

19th century, however, man's attitude towards the sea was changing. Coastal communities began turning to fishing realising, at the same time, that they could turn to their advantage the misfortunes of mariners by attempting to salvage something from the wrecked ships.

Between the years 1866 and 1875 nearly 10,000 ships, excluding fishing vessels, were wrecked, the great majority of these being collier brigs on their way to and from the Tyne.

Despite all these problems the average 19th century skipper was a man to be admired, having learned his trade the hard way by starting as a boy and working his way up. The problems he had to overcome during this period would have made many give up. Charts of the North Sea did not exist before 1847, and even then the information they conveyed was very basic. There was no substitute for experience when navigating the shallow waters of what has been described as the most treacherous sea in the world.

It was against this background of shipwreck and loss of life that, towards the latter part of the 18th century, the fishermen within the coastal communities formed themselves into groups, known as beach companies, for the purpose of salvage and rescue at sea, an occupation that in the mid-19th century produced rich rewards.

These companies, usually comprising 30 or 40 men, were governed by strict sets of rules and regulations, the members of the company owning shares in company property and receiving a share of the salvage money, "doled" out according to their rule book. The opening words of the rule book for the Caister Company read as follows:

"THE CAISTER COMPANY OF BEACHMEN, formed for the purpose of saving property, and of rendering assistance to vessels or ships aground, stranded or wrecked on the sands or beach, or in any kind of difficulty, distress or disaster at sea, consists of Forty Shareholders, having an equal share, right, and interest in certain boats, boat-house or shed, tackling, etc, lying and being in the Parish of Caister next Great Yarmouth in the County of Norfolk.

The remuneration, earnings, and emoluments arising from any such services shall be divided and apportioned in certain shares for the maintenance of the boats belonging to the Company, and amongst those members of the Company who shall be entitled to share in any such earnings, under and according to the following RULES AND REGULATIONS."

There then followed a detailed set of rules covering all aspects of the work.

Almost every seaside village from Aldeburgh in the south to Mundesley in the north supported such a company, each with its own high lookout on the beach or cliff, each with its own boats known as yawls and gigs with which men could quickly respond to a vessel in distress. This speed was not necessarily for the benefit of those unfortunate enough to be in trouble at sea, but because the laws of salvage at sea weigh heavily in favour of the first boat to reach the scene and offer assistance.

The Caister company was founded about 1790, and with fishing formed the main source of income for many families in a village with a population of less than 500. The majority, however, were more concerned with obtaining a living from agriculture than the sea.

The fortunes of the beach company were reflected in the value of the shares as they changed hands throughout the years. A typical example of these changing values can be seen by following the somewhat unusual course of one particular share, owned by William George of Caister.

When he died in 1864 his widow, Maria, sold it for £95, a substantial sum in the 19th century. It is difficult to compare this with today's prices as values have changed considerably since the 1860s, but it is interesting to note that in 1864 the average agricultural wage was 11s 0d (55p).

The purchaser of the share was Benjamin Barnard of Scratby, a member of the California beach company, who took the opportunity to move south and join a more prosperous company. Benjamin died in 1882, and four years later his widow, Emma, for reasons unknown, was declared bankrupt, the share having been used as security for a £12 loan from Yarmouth solicitor Harold Chamberlain. Chamberlain was now able to buy the share from the Official Receiver for the bargain price of

'Covent Garden' (1899-1919) A 40' boat of the Norfolk and Suffolk design it required a crew of 14 men. Picture c1905.

£5, and after keeping it for two years sold it to John Samuel "Sprat" Haylett for £15.

In just over 20 years the share had been devalued by some 80 per cent, an indication of the falling fortunes of beach companies now suffering from the introduction of steam tugs, better navigation and iron ships. In 1927 the same share was only worth £5 when sold to Robert Haylett, landlord of the Ship Inn.

Salvage work was now only a small part of a beachman's work, although the ownership of a share still produced a reasonable income for many people.

Lifeboats were introduced along the coastline during the early years of the 19th century, and from the beach companies came the men to form the crews. These early sailing and pulling lifeboats were far removed from the later self righting boats, and the business of life saving was risky for the rescued and the rescuer. Other facilities which were being developed at this time included the rocket apparatus of Captain Manby, the Yarmouth barrack master. This was operated by the coastguard service, a group originally set up to combat smuggling, which was expanded in the 19th century to include life saving among its duties.

Lowestoft had the first lifeboat on the east coast in 1801. Yarmouth had one by 1825, and Caister received its first lifeboat in 1845. The beachmen could now provide a more efficient service to seafarers while still being able to make a living from salvage work. However, it became necessary for the various life saving societies which provided the lifeboats to institute a reward scheme to encourage the beachmen to put to sea when life saving was the only possibility. Their livelihood, after all, came from salvage work.

The first Caister lifeboat was transferred to the village from Bacton by the Norfolk Shipwreck Association, but it proved unsatisfactory. The following year, after a public subscription, a new boat was built at the Yarmouth yard of Branford for the Caister station and put into service in 1846. This boat was in use until 1865, during which time the RNLI had taken over responsibility for many boats along the east coast, including Caister, a responsibility it was to hold in the village until 1969.

There were to be many lifeboats stationed at Caister during the RNLI years, boats that performed many heroic services, some of which were recognised by the Institution when they presented their coveted gold and silver medals for outstanding service to members of the crews.

In 1875 the coxswain, Philip George, was awarded the silver medal for a rescue which involved the lifeboat crew but not the lifeboat. The schooner *Wild Wave* of Sunderland ran on to Caister beach after fouling the Cockle Sands. Two members of the schooner's crew, the master and a boy, were drowned when they were washed off the rigging by heavy seas, but the beachmen managed to get through the surf and rescue the three remaining members of the crew. In addition to recognising the courage of the coxswain, the RNLI gave £10 to all who had taken part in the rescue.

The Caister beachmen receiving instruction in navigation from a retired sea Captain (in the bowler hat), Captain Allen, c1910. In the background are the lifeboats 'Covent Garden' and 'Nancy Lucy'. (Mrs V Thacker)

Local people also recognised the bravery of their beachmen, and the following January each one of the 40 members of the company received four guineas, presented to them in blue satin bags, the result of a public subscription raised "as a testimonial for their bravery at the wreck of the *Wild Wave* and many other acts of daring in rescuing shipwrecked crews."

This tradition of lifeboat work was kept alive by successive generations of beachmen, and during the period the RNLI maintained the lifeboat at Caister the station saved 1815 lives, a record not exceeded by any other station in the British Isles.

It was this tradition that was to be so influential in the life and work of John Woodhouse.

SKIPJACK

When the wind shifts against the sun
Trust it not for it will rain.

John Joseph Woodhouse was born on November 10, 1912, the first child of Joseph and Annabella Woodhouse, in a cottage only a few yards from where he still lives today in the heart of the old beachmen's "village." He grew up in a family where the main topic of conversation was always connected with the sea, mainly fishing or lifeboats. Given this background it is not surprising that from a very early age the boy took a keen interest in such matters himself. It was an interest that was to overshadow all the usual activities and interests of young boys.

During the first world war, and with father away in the Navy, the family moved in with an uncle invalided out of the Army who was also a member of the village lifeboat launching party, and the call-out man. This latter job entailed going round the houses of the crew to make sure they had heard the call-out bell, a very necessary job on a stormy winter's night when wind and rain would easily deaden the sound of the bell being frantically rung from the beach look-out. As a young boy, John would help his uncle.

"As a boy I used to have to run round the village and help gather the crew. You see, there were several who were quite hard of hearing and they hadn't a clue when the bell sounded. It didn't matter what time of day it was, we'd still have to round them up. If it was in the middle of the night we'd have to knock 'em up."

This job sometimes had its lighter moments, like the occasion when he called coxswain "Sprat" Haylett to launch the boat after the lookout had seen a submarine aground on a sand bank. "Sprat" would not consider launching the lifeboat until a message had been sent to the coastguard, asking them to signal the submarine with a Morse lamp to make sure it was not an enemy boat.

On another occasion young John had to suffer the wrath of his grandfather. "I saw a light on in a downstairs room at his house so I guessed he must have heard the bell. I chased off to another house and left him. But in fact the light was on because of a lodger he had sleeping in the room. The boat was launched without him, and that night the crew got paid salvage - and that was rare in 1928. The last one had been years before. And I can tell you, he wasn't at all happy."

School was not one of young John's favourite pastimes, and he could not wait for the school day to finish so he could get down to the beach to be with the beachmen. While his friends played football or other games, John was on the beach listening to the tales of the old beachmen or helping where he could with the fishing boats, hoping that someone would offer to take him with them on a fishing trip that

John Woodhouse at the age of 12 with his sister Irene, who died as a young girl.

evening. Breakfast time, lunch time, evenings, in fact any time he was not required at school, he could be found on the beach.

Many hours were passed in the old beach company lookout. When the call-out bell was rung he would be one of the first on to the beach, helping to push the heavy lifeboat down the beach, looking forward to the day when he could join the crew.

These early lifeboats could weigh up to 10 tons and needed at least 20 people to launch them by pushing the boat down to the sea on rollers, or "skeets." When in the breakers, the boat would be hauled off by the crew pulling on the "haul off rope," a rope anchored some 150 fathoms out to sea and being pulled over a roller on the bow of the boat. At the same time the shore party would use the "set pole," a long pole pushed against the stern of the boat.

"SKIPJACK"

It was while at the village school in Beach Road, itself only about 200 yards from the beach, that John acquired the nickname "Skipper." This was not through his seafaring capabilities, for he was still far too young, but because his uncle had given him a sailor's cap he had obtained from a rescued seaman which had the name Skipjack on the ribbon. John wore the cap every day, and it was not long before even his family were calling him "Skipper," a name that has stayed with him ever since.

Formal education finished for "Skipper" at the age of 14. He could then spend all his time on the beach. But now he had to turn his hand to making a living.

One of his first jobs was shrimping off the beach with a push net. After making his catch he would take the shrimps home and boil them in the wash house copper ready for the customers, of which there never seemed to be a shortage. Many village people would call at the house during the day, leaving a bowl or dish with a note in it saying how many shrimps they wanted. The utensils would be filled when the catch was boiled.

Another way he found to make a few shillings was to take a barrow around the village selling herring and mackerel the local fishermen had caught. For this he was paid a commission of 2d for every shilling's worth of fish sold.

By the time "Skipper" was born the English seaside resort had become an established institution, and the village of Caister took its

The "Skipjack" cap that gave young John the nickname that has been with him since his schooldays.

A Woodhouse family group c1930. In the deckchairs are father and grandfather while in the centre is "Skipper" with cousin Sydney on the left.

share of summer visitors from the nearby popular resort of Great Yarmouth.

The fashion for sea bathing had grown up among the aristocracy and gentry during the middle years of the 18th century, when sea water was prescribed as a cure for a variety of medical conditions. Strange as it may seem today in these times of pollution of our seas, many doctors encouraged people to drink the water, sometimes in enormous quantities. By the late 19th century the seaside had become the playground of the working classes from the industrial Midlands, the railways having opened up areas which were hitherto almost inaccessible to most people. For many fishing villages the resort element became an important part of the economy.

Caister moved into this new "industry" late in the century when the privately owned Manor House, an imposing building standing on the cliffs, was purchased by a property company and converted into an hotel. The hotel had its own golf course, an important facility at that period when participant sports were becoming increasingly popular, and a seaside holiday provided excellent opportunities for polishing one's skills. By the 1890s golf was the "in" game, and by the turn of the century almost every seaside resort was in easy reach of a golf course. The Manor House Hotel catered for the more fastidious visitor, and its guests included many members of the legal and financial worlds.

The Camp catered for another type of holidaymaker. Established in 1906 at the northern end of the village, it offered a week's holiday for two guineas which included all meals and transport from the railway station. The prospectus for 1924 expounded the pleasures of camping: "one can have the pleasure of camp life without its discomforts; live the simple open air life free from cramping conditions of the ordinary house, while enjoying the comforts of well equipped tents and huts." This 30 acre camp site extended to the beach and provided local beachmen with a plentiful supply of visitors eager to sample the experience of a sea trip.

For those holidaymakers who preferred to stay in a house and not in a "well-equipped tent or hut," there was the apartment, the fore-runner of today's bed and breakfast type of accommodation. Many households in the village, including those of the fishing families, shared their houses with visitors in the summer months, and the sign, "Apartments to Let," was a common sight in the windows.

The Woodhouse family, now enlarged with Rose, born in 1921, David, seven years later, and a resident aunt and uncle, found room to accommodate visitors in common with many beachmen's families. The extra income was very useful at a time of the year when fishing was at its slackest, and while the wives looked after the guests, with the help of any other female members of the family, the menfolk took the opportunity to make a few shillings from sea tripping or deck chair hire.

Deck chairs could be hired on the beach for 2d per morning session and 2d for the afternoon, and these were owned by a man known

Summer 1899 and a group of beachmen, with "Jimmy" Haylett on the left, pass the time of day with a group of holidaymakers outside the beach hut. (Ken Jary)

19

The 'Endeavour', built for "Skipper" in 1934, the boat with which he revived the "tripping" business from Caister beach.

as "Mab" Brown who engaged young "Skipper" to look after them and collect the money. At the end of each week he would receive a half share of the takings, which in a good week could amount to a respectable 7s 6d (37½p). This type of seasonal job was undertaken by beachmen on many beaches along the coastline where there were holidaymakers, and is an example of how they turned their hands to every opportunity to supplement their income from any beach related activity that might arise.

"Skipper" had not worked for "Mab" long before the old chap died. Afraid to take the money round to his house at the end of that week, "Skipper" waited until the following week before venturing to give it to "Mab's" widow. "Why didn't you come last week?" she chastised him. "We could have done with that." "Skipper" informed her he had a few broken chairs as well. As this was the height of the season, and looking for the maximum income, the old lady promptly took up a section of stair carpet for him to mend the torn chairs. Every penny was important to the beachmen's families in those days.

The apartment system of accommodation differed from today's bed and breakfast in that guests provided all their own food, to be cooked for them by the lady of the house. They were usually charged 10 shillings for the room and £2 per week for the services of having food cooked and hot water provided. Many people returned to the same family year after year for their holiday. A local guide to the village was published in 1926, and many people advertised their apartments, such as: "Mrs W Haylett, Sunnyside, 3 bedrooms and 2 sitting rooms; attendance."

Many also offered the use of a beach hut or tent as an additional amenity, and visitors were also catered for by Refreshment Rooms and Tea Rooms in other parts of the village. Take-away food was available from the fried fish and chipped potato shop, and the holidaymaker to Caister could also enjoy a farm holiday where the farm house offered every comfort with milk, butter and poultry "fresh from the farm."

The small village of Caister had by now become firmly established as a holiday centre, and the guide book described it as:

Not an assertive place at any time, the small voice of Caister-on-Sea is not infrequently unheard by those holiday makers who search each year for an idyllic little seaside place wherein they can find infinitude of peace, and such surroundings as will prove mentally refreshing and conducive of the creation of a peaceful mind.

In the days before the motor car a majority of visitors, having arrived by train, stayed in the village for the duration of their holiday and spent most of their time on the beach, although there was easy access to Great Yarmouth by the tramway, opened in 1907. In 1923 a brisk trade was made by the beachmen by taking sightseers out to the Scroby Sands, at 2s 6d (12½p) per person, to see the wreck of the 1300 ton steamer *Hopelyn*, driven on to the sands in the gales of the previous October.

By carefully saving the money earned from shrimping and his other odd jobs, "Skipper" was able to buy his first boat in 1929, an ex-drifter's lifeboat called the *Dashing Spray*. He was now 16, and with the help of his father he obtained a few nets and was able to start fishing in his own boat. During the summer months the boat was used to take visitors sailing and fishing.

Caister beach with the beachmen's lookout and the bathing hut.

"SKIPPER" JACK

After a few years the money earned was invested in a new motor boat, built in the village, named *Endeavour*. With this, "Skipper" revived the tripping business, taking parties to the Cockle lightship when the weather was suitable, sharing the work with another boat, the *Rainbow*, which was also working off Caister beach. When the tripping was slow the boat was used for shrimping, and throughout the winter months, fishing.

By the 1930s the village had grown considerably with a resident population of over 2500. The holiday industry continued to expand, with camping grounds being opened where visitors were accommodated in wooden chalets - the forerunners of today's caravan camps.

As soon as David was old enough he started to help "Skipper," and the two brothers worked together at the combination of tripping during the holiday season and fishing for the rest of the year.

David had first gone to sea at the age of four when he accompanied "Skipper" on trips to see *HMS Warspite*, anchored off Britannia Pier on a goodwill visit. When he left school he followed the family's traditional occupation, taking the place of their uncle Jack, who had now reached retiring age.

This was to be the pattern of their life for many years, although the requirements of visitors to the village did eventually change. The sea trip aspect of their work declined, and eventually died out completely in the 1980s.

FAMILY BACKGROUND

When the sun goes down beneath the black
A westerly wind you may expect.

In the early years of the 19th century the Caister beach company was strengthened by a steady influx of experienced beachmen from villages to the north, particularly Winterton, a seafaring community some six miles along the coast. Winterton had for long been recognised as the home of some of the most experienced seamen on the Norfolk coast. They were the men who skippered a majority of the Yarmouth fishing boats at the height of the fortunes of the herring industry, and the men who became coxswains of many lifeboats along this section of coast.

These men, with their families, migrated southwards during the first half of the 19th century mainly to cut down the travelling distance to Yarmouth. As they moved south they formed new communities at Newport and California, and increased the population of the established village of Caister. Names such as Brown, Haylett and Hodds soon became well known all along the coastline. They were names that were to be associated with lifeboat and beach company work for generations to come.

This influx of people into Caister necessitated new development, and houses were built on land between the old village and the sea, land that had previously been waste sand dunes. Clay Road and the eastern end of Beach Road formed the nucleus of this development, and the pebble built cottages soon became a beachmen's "village," a separate community complete with its own public house, the Ship Inn, built in 1815 for Robert George, one of the first of the men to come from Winterton.

Winterton-born men had, by mid-century, all but taken over the Caister beach company, their expertise strengthening and making it one of the most successful along this stretch of coastline.

Among the many who migrated south were members of the Haylett family, whose ancestral tree can be traced to 1508, with tentative connections back to the 14th century. In the 16th century one member of the Haylett family was appointed bailiff of Yarmouth on two separate occasions, the bailiff being the equivalent in local government office to today's mayor. This was Christopher Heylott, by trade a worstead weaver, and brother of Thomas, from whom the line of this book descends.

These early members of the family lived in the Norfolk villages of Lessingham and Happisburgh, and by the early 17th century had moved to Palling with occupations such as yeoman, husbandman and blacksmith, indicating that not all of them were seafaring folk. By the

"SKIPPER" JACK

The flint pebble cottages on the right were built for the beachmen in the 1840s and it was in this row that "Skipper" was born and has lived all his life.

end of the century the family-tree had moved to Winterton, and mariner and fisherman began to appear. One of the earliest in the line connected with the sea was Samuel, born in 1694.

Two members of this Haylett family form the roots of part of a large family tree whose branches reach out to include the Browns, the Knights and the Woodhouses.

Isaiah Haylett, born in 1827, and his brother James, born 1824, spent their early years in Winterton, but as young men they moved their families south to Caister. By 1852 James had bought himself a share in the Caister beach company, and both men soon became prominent members of the beach community.

Isaiah had a family of nine - Martha, Robina, Sarah, Charles ("Stow"), Henry ("Squay"), Benjamin ("Titabee"), John Samuel ("Sprat"), Josiah and William. Nicknames were essential in a community where many people shared the same surname. In 1889 Martha married Joseph Woodhouse of Hemsby, from a family which had originated in the small farming village of Thrigby, some four miles inland. From this marriage of Martha and Joseph was born a son, in 1889, again given the family name Joseph. He was to become "Skipper's" father.

Isaiah's brother James ("Jimmy") Haylett had a family of eight children - James, George, Aaron, Frederick, Walter, Damaris, Sarah and Emma. Sarah married into the Brown family, the groom being Robert ("Puddens"), son of Solomon ("Gundy") Brown, who had been awarded a medal of the Grand Duke of Mecklenburg in 1868 while a member of

24

the California beach company. Mecklenburg was a Grand Duchy state of 19th century North Germany, situated on the Baltic coast. The son of Sarah and Robert, whose nickname was "Sequah," became coxswain of the Caister lifeboat for the period 1950 until 1956.

The other daughter of James Haylett, Emma, married Charles Knights, one of the three survivors of the *Beauchamp* lifeboat disaster of 1901. Of the six boys, three were lost in lifeboat service, two in the *Beauchamp* and one, Frederick, in a yawl accident in 1885. James, one of the two lost in the *Beauchamp*, and the coxswain from 1887, had a daughter, Annabella Victoria, born in 1887, and in 1912 she married Joseph Woodhouse, a second cousin from Isaiah's side of the family.

From this somewhat complex family tree we have now arrived at "Skipper's" parents.

One final family tie that should be included in this record is that of James Haylett, junior, "Skipper's" grandfather, who married Mary Ann Brett, a descendant of Benjamin Hodds, first coxswain of the Caister lifeboat and a stalwart member of the beach company in the early 19th century.

From an early period these beachmen had to come to terms with the harsh realities of their dangerous profession, and the Haylett family featured prominently in a yawl catastrophe which happened on the night of July 21, 1885. Fifteen beachmen put off in their yawl, *Zephyr*, to go to the aid of a schooner stranded on the Barber Sands. About a mile from the shore they hit the mast of a wreck, a pure accident, as the crew were well aware of the old mast and the coxswain had called out, "Look out for the wreck," as they approached the spot. The yawl began to fill with water, and the crew found themselves in the sea. One crewman swam for the shore, and on the way attracted the attention of a shrimper

Caister beach c1910.

25

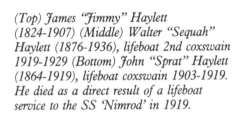

(Top) James "Jimmy" Haylett
(1824-1907) (Middle) Walter "Sequah"
Haylett (1876-1936), lifeboat 2nd coxswain
1919-1929 (Bottom) John "Sprat" Haylett
(1864-1919), lifeboat coxswain 1903-1919.
He died as a direct result of a lifeboat
service to the SS 'Nimrod' in 1919.

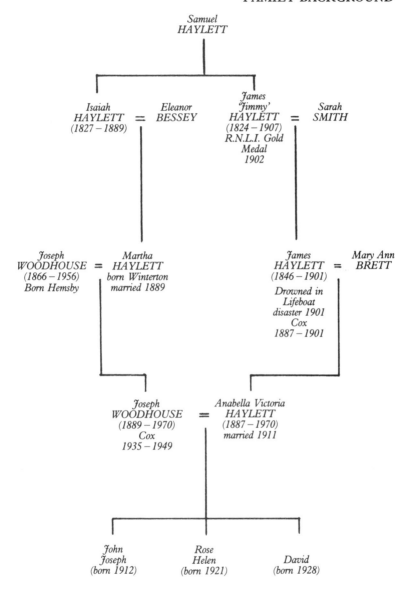

WOODHOUSE/HAYLETT RELATIONSHIP

who immediately went to the aid of the stricken beachmen.

The small shrimp boat managed to save six of the yawl's crew, but the remaining eight were drowned. Of the men saved four were from the Haylett family, while another two Hayletts were among those drowned. The incident illustrates how tragedy can strike during comparatively calm weather in mid-summer, and the devastating effect it could have on a family in which so many members followed the same occupation.

The lifeboat tales these men could recall were legion, many being passed from one generation to the next. Stories of bravery and seamanship, like the experience of Joseph Woodhouse on October 31, 1891, when the small lifeboat *Godsend* was launched to go to the aid of a barge, the *Brightlingsea* of Harwich, aground on Haisboro' Sands a few miles north of Caister. As a strong northerly gale was blowing the lifeboat engaged a steam tug to tow them to the sands, a common practice at that time. The seas were so rough that the powerful tug pulled the small boat through the waves at an alarming rate, the situation becoming so dangerous that a crew member had to be stationed at the bow of the lifeboat with an axe, ready to cut the tow if there was a danger that the boat would be pulled under.

When they eventually reached the sands they found the larger lifeboats from Winterton and Palling already on the scene, but not prepared to go into the wreck because of the shallow waters. The *Godsend* released the tow and the crew rowed to the sunken barge where they found the exhausted crew clinging to the wreckage. On this occasion the lifeboat saved four lives.

The Caister lifeboat disaster of 1901 had a devastating effect on the lives of many people in the village when in one night nine lifeboat-men were drowned only a few hundred yards from their own lifeboat shed. The Haylett family was again in the midst of a disaster, as they had been in 1885, and the fact that Jimmy Haylett was awarded the RNLI gold medal for his part in the rescue attempts on this occasion did nothing to compensate for the loss of his son and grandson. A bitter blow to one family.

The lifeboat *Beauchamp*, stationed at Caister since 1892, was at the centre of this tragedy.

Just after 11pm on the night of November 13, 1901, the Caister watch saw flares from the vicinity of the Barber Sands. The signal was acknowledged by the Cockle lightship firing guns and rockets at regular intervals, and the men on the beach quickly realised that the lifeboat was needed. There were two lifeboats to choose from, and it was decided that the smaller boat with the shallow draft was the most suitable in spite of the rough seas.

With great difficulty the *Beauchamp* was launched into the surf, only to be washed up on the beach again, broadside on. The seas worsened as for three hours the men struggled to relaunch the boat in intense darkness and driving rain. Finally, at about 2am, with the aid of

The crew of the No. 2 lifeboat c1896. Back row, from the left: Frank Clowes (Hon Secretary), Solly Brown, Charles Sneller, Billy Read, Jimmy Haylett. Centre row: Billy Wilson, Jimmy Haylett, Walter Haylett. Front row: George Haylett, Harry Knights, Joe Julier, Ben Kittle.

warp and tackle, the boat was successfully launched. It quickly disappeared into the dark night. Many of the launching crew went home to change out of their wet clothes, but Jimmy Haylett, aged 78, with two sons, two grandsons and a son-in-law all part of the crew that night, remained on watch in the lifeboat house.

An hour had passed when Frederick Haylett, returning to the beach after changing his clothes, heard cries coming from the water's edge. With old Jimmy he ran to the scene. To their horror they saw the *Beauchamp* keel up in the surf with the sea breaking over her hull. Apparently the boat, after having left the beach, had sailed towards the Caister Shoal and started to tack. On the second of these manoeuvres the boat refused to go about, and although the sails were quickly lowered the crew could not avoid the boat coming broadside to the sea and capsizing in the surf.

The two Hayletts ran into the water to look for survivors, realizing the seriousness of the situation. Jimmy found his son-in-law struggling to get clear of the upturned boat, and quickly helped him to the beach before returning into the water to rescue one of his grandsons, Walter Haylett. Meanwhile, Fred had brought another crew member, John Hubbard, to the safety of the beach. Coastguards and rocket apparatus had now arrived on the scene, but little more could be done. They could only watch as, at intervals, bodies were washed from under

29

the boat. The next day the storm abated and by mid-day an attempt was made to right the boat. When this was done three more bodies were found in the wreckage.

In all, nine members of the beach company were lost in the disaster, an event that attracted national publicity and brought into prominence the gallantry of the Caister men. One of those lost was James Haylett, junior, "Skipper's" grandfather, who had taken over the job of coxswain in 1886 and after a few years had relinquished the post in favour of his brother, Aaron. Both these men, together with their father and another brother, Frederick, were all in the earlier disaster when the yawl *Zephyr* foundered on July 21, 1885, with the loss of eight lives.

A sad epilogue to this story emerged later. The Lowestoft smack the lifeboat had been launched to assist had not made a distress signal in the first place. The skipper had lit a flare when his navigation light had gone out and anchored inside the sand bank for the night. At first light the smack sailed away on its journey unaware of the drama on the beach during the night.

The Board of Trade inquiry subsequently held at Yarmouth Town Hall looked in great detail at the events leading up to the disaster, and came to the conclusions that the accident was in no way due to any defect in the boat, nor to any mismanagement on the part of the crew. As one witness remarked, "under similar circumstances anything could have gone over."

It is often quoted that Jimmy Haylett said, "Caister men never turn back," at the inquest held into this disaster, but this is not quite

The 'Beauchamp' the morning after the tragedy of November 1901 when nine members of the crew were drowned.

30

correct. What really happened was that the Coroner asked whether the lifeboatmen had given the ship up, meaning had they realised they were on a hopeless task. Jimmy Haylett replied, without hesitation, "No sir, they would never give up. It's against our rules." And a juryman chimed in with, "They are not born that sort here." The phrase, "never turn back" has, however, become synonymous with the Caister lifeboat, and is today immortalised by a public house of that name.

This incident had a devastating effect. Forty-one children were left fatherless, and the whole village mourned. Almost every beachman's family had lost a relative, and curtains and blinds were drawn while the church bell tolled throughout the dreary November afternoon. The funeral, held the following Sunday, was a moving scene as thousands thronged the streets to see the eight horse-drawn hearses make their way to the church where lifeboatmen from many other villages had gathered with Scottish fishermen, the district MP, Sir Edward Birbeck, and many local dignitaries, to pay their last respects to the gallant men.

On the night of January 29, 1919, the *S S Nimrod*, a ship at one time owned by that great explorer, Sir Ernest Shackleton, went aground on Barber Sands. The *Nimrod* fired distress signals which were immediately followed by signals from the Cockle lightship. Despite high seas and snow, the Caister men launched their boat, but it was thrown back broadside on to the beach. Soaked to the skin and almost frozen with cold the crew struggled and fought the waves until at last they succeeded in getting the boat afloat again. When they were within hailing distance of the steamer the ship's lights suddenly went out. Failing to get alongside, and since there were no signs of life aboard, the lifeboat sailed to the Cockle lightship, only to learn that they had not picked anyone up, either.

The lifeboat sailed to Winterton searching the black seas without success, and at 3am, after being at sea for over three hours, they returned and anchored near the wreck. Daylight revealed only two masts and the top of a funnel visible, and the lifeboat decided to return home. It reached Caister beach at 8.30am with the crew suffering from exposure. Two of the *Nimrod's* crew were washed ashore, alive, in a small boat to the south of the village, but one died two days later. The captain was washed ashore at California, dead. Coxswain John Haylett, of the Caister lifeboat, never fully recovered from the long ordeal at sea and died five weeks later.

"Skipper's" father, Joseph, like many of his family before him, had gone to sea at an early age. In 1910 he joined the Caister beach company and sailed with the lifeboat whenever possible, his first rescue service being on January 11, 1912, when the lifeboat *Covent Garden* saved seven members of the crew of the German schooner *Falke*. At the outbreak of the war in 1914 he went to Birmingham to work in a munitions factory, but the call of the sea was strong and he soon returned, joining the Navy and becoming a mate on a trawler.

After the war he returned to fishing, becoming a skipper in 1928,

"SKIPPER" JACK

"Skipper's" father Joe Woodhouse, lifeboat coxswain 1935-1949.

but in 1931 gave up the sea to work ashore. Still an active member of the beach company, he became coxswain of the lifeboat in 1935, a position he held for 14 years.

"Skipper" clearly remembers May 25, 1940, when he was a crew member, and his father the coxswain, as the lifeboat was called out to the *Charles Boyes*, a trawler blown up by a mine near Cockle Sands. When they reached the scene they found only two survivors, one clinging to a lifebuoy, the other to a lifebelt. Both were taken aboard the lifeboat, which continued to tack among the debris until the Gorleston boat arrived on the scene. The Caister boat then returned to the beach to land the injured men. It was discovered later that among those lost on the trawler were two members of the Caister beach company.

This was to be the last service of the sailing lifeboat *Charles Burton*, the last lifeboat to rescue life under sail along the East Anglian coast. With the arrival of the replacement boat, a motor boat, the *Jose Nevillè*, in 1941, the beachmen decided times had changed so much that it was now time to disband the beach company. It had survived longer that most. The Caister beachmen now concentrated on running a lifeboat service.

LIFEBOATS

At sea with a low and falling glass
Soundly sleeps a careless ass
Only when it's low and rising
Soundly sleeps a careful wise one.

As already mentioned in the first chapter, lifeboats had been stationed at Caister since 1845, and over the years members of the beach company made many heroic and daring rescues.

"Skipper" Woodhouse had his first experience of a trip in the lifeboat in 1921, when he was only nine years old. At that time there were two lifeboats stationed at the village, the *James Leath* and the *Nancy Lucy*, both of the Norfolk and Suffolk design, a type favoured by the local beachmen. They were powered by 12 oars and sail. The *James Leath* was a 42-foot boat, and the *Nancy Lucy* slightly smaller, being 35 feet long.

By 1927 the last of the beach company yawls had been sold. All salvage work had to be undertaken with the RNLI lifeboats. The Institution ruled that its lifeboats were not to be used to save property, except when no other aid was available. On those occasions where this was the case the crew could perform salvage services on condition that a sum equal to two shares was paid to the Institution "to cover risk of damage to the boats." By this date, however, the salvage aspect of beachmen's work had diminished greatly, and life saving was at the fore.

Speed had always been essential in any salvage or rescue service. The beach yawls were ideal, but in 1928 Caister men proved that a lifeboat could be just as fast. In gale force winds gusting up to 100 miles per hour the *James Leath* was launched to go to the aid of a Lowestoft smack, the *Forget-me-not*. The crew used the haul-off rope to clear the beach and were about to hoist sail when the coxswain realised the wind was with them. He decided the boat was already going too fast. Without sail, they covered the 2½ miles to Scroby Sand in about 10 minutes, an incredible speed.

In 1929 the RNLI closed one of the Caister stations by transferring the *James Leath* to Aldeburgh. The *Nancy Lucy* was replaced by the *Charles Burton*, a Liverpool type boat of 14 oars brought from Grimsby, and this boat was to remain at Caister for the next 12 years and was to have the distinction of being the last lifeboat to complete a.rescue under sail. Motor lifeboats had slowly replaced all the sailing boats around the coast by the early 1940s.

It was mentioned earlier that the beach company was governed by a strict set of rules and regulations, and it was one of these rules that gave "Skipper," then aged 20, his first opportunity to become one of the company, an ambition he had nurtured for many years. Rule VII stated:

"SKIPPER" JACK

The lifeboats 'Nancy Lucy' and 'Covent Garden' c1910.

The widow or children of any deceased member of the Company shall, in all cases, be allowed to put a man into the Company to work, provided always the man proposed shall be considered fit and suitable person, and approved by the Company or the majority thereof.

The neighbour and good friend of the Woodhouse family, Will Green, died in March, 1933, and in accordance with the rule his widow looked for somebody to work Will's share for her. Many widows had made the mistake of asking a fishing boat skipper to work their share, but to their cost found that the fisherman was away more than at home, thus missing the majority of lifeboat launches. Who better for Will's widow to ask than her young neighbour? He was a person she knew would be accepted by the Company, and a person who fished from the Caister beach and was always available when the call-out bell was rung.

A widow's share entitled the man who worked it to retain three-quarters of the money earned, the widow receiving the other quarter, a system that seemed to be agreeable to all concerned. "Skipper" was now the youngest member of the company, which consisted of 39 men, one share having laid dormant for several years.

The first occasion "Skipper" became part of the lifeboat crew was at a practice launch a few months later when, with the RNLI inspector aboard and in rough weather, the boat was hauled off with the warp and then pulled ashore again, not a dramatic rescue mission but one of the many routine launchings the company had to make to make sure the crew would respond well when a real emergency happened.

Lifeboatman
"Skipper"
Woodhouse.

The following August the crew was called out to assist a fishing boat in trouble, and nearly got into difficulties themselves. The Gorleston and Lowestoft lifeboats were out of service and the Caister boat was covering the whole area when a message was received at 7am to launch for a boat in trouble some two miles to the north. With the help of several holidaymakers they launched in a heavy swell with a good wind, and were soon under sail. When they reached the fishing boat they dropped an anchor and got a line aboard. The anchor did not hold, and the crew had to take to the oars to row for 20 minutes to get back to the boat in trouble. The fishermen had to jump into the lifeboat and pull up the sails while the lifeboat crew kept rowing, eventually getting their boat clear of the wreck to sail back to the beach.

This also happened to be the annual lifeboat day, and when they reached the beach many people thought the rescue had been an arranged display, not realising the problems the crew had just experienced. This type of incident was hard work for the 17 men in a rowing lifeboat, but would have caused no problems at all for a motor lifeboat.

"SKIPPER" JACK

A group of four pictures showing the launching routine of the sailing lifeboat 'Covent Garden'. (Mrs G Haylett)

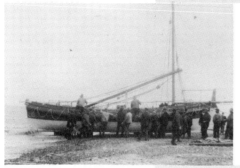

In January, 1935, the lifeboat was at sea for some 24 hours, going to the assistance of the trawler *Prosper*, of Ostend.

The day had begun early for "Skipper" who, with his uncle, had intended to go fishing and had started to bait up their lines before daylight. The southerly wind began to freshen, and it was decided the fishing would have to be cancelled when the lifeboat coxswain, Charles Laycock, arrived to say the coastguards had noticed a boat stationary since before midnight, but not, in their opinion, aground. The coastguards had only recently moved their lookout from Caister to a new position on Britannia Pier at Yarmouth, and the Caister men were sceptical of the judgements they sometimes made.

At first light "Skipper" and the coxswain were in the old look-out shed, and decided that the trawler was aground on Scroby Sands, probably having fouled its propeller. After a short consultation they decided to launch their lifeboat, and the call-out bell was rung although the trawler was out of their area and they risked a confrontation with the Gorleston lifeboat. The bell rang at the same time as the local children were going to school, and this caused a worthwhile diversion for many of them to help launch the lifeboat.

The boat was launched and a tow rope thrown ashore. The beach party, consisting of many children, pulled the boat along while the crew on board hoisted the sails. When they reached the Caister/Yarmouth boundary the tow was released and the lifeboat quickly sailed away towards Scroby and the stranded trawler.

When they arrived at the scene the skipper accepted their help just as the Gorleston lifeboat arrived and, as expected, complained that the Caister boat was out of its area. Despite this, the Caister boat laid an anchor for the trawler and engaged two tugs which had also arrived at the scene. But their efforts to free the stricken boat failed. The wind backed southerly and strengthened, and the trawler skipper was told to pump out the fresh water tanks and unload the briquettes (used instead of coal to fuel the boilers) from the bunker to a position under the forecastle in an effort to lift the stern. This arduous task was completed by 14 lifeboatmen and 14 of the Belgian crew, the lifeboat coxswain and the bowman staying with their boat. The following day, on the flood tide, the boat floated off the sands with the assistance of the Yarmouth tug *Tackfull*. The lifeboat then took over and towed it into harbour. Three crew members were left on board the trawler while the remainder sailed the lifeboat back to Caister, a relatively easy task with the wind off the land, although it was freezing hard.

We saw earlier how the rules of the beach company allowed "Skipper" to gain a foothold in the system by working a widow's share. In 1936 a change in the rules gave him the opportunity to become a fully fledged member by owning his own share.

It had been a company rule that if a man was injured while working for the company he was allowed to keep his full share for a year and thereafter receive a half share of the earnings of the company, a form

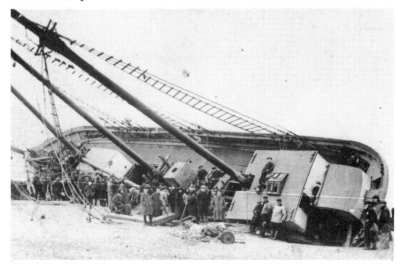

The 'Moorside', a three masted schooner wrecked on Caister beach in 1919. The wreck was bought by the local blacksmith for scrap. The crew were saved by the Caister Rocket Company.

of disability pension in the years before the welfare state existed. A company meeting in 1936 amended this rule so that the person would either have to sell his share or find somebody to work it for him, in a similar arrangement to widows. This change was necessary to ensure that there were enough working members of the company, because a situation had arisen where outside people had to be asked to make up a crew. The sailing lifeboat needed a crew of 17, 14 of whom were required to row.

One of the men affected by this change in policy was Jimmy Bultitude, a Caister man injured some years previously at a lifeboat launch. He decided to sell his share, and when "Skipper" heard this he decided it was the opportunity he had been waiting for. He purchased the share for £2 10s (£2.50). The value of beach company shares had reached an all time low by this date, but there was still enough salvage work to make it worthwhile to be a member. Although he had worked a share for three years, and had been known to the men of the company since boyhood, "Skipper" still had to go through the laid down procedure of being re-accepted, which in this case proved to be a mere formality. The widow's share he had previously worked passed to another Caister man, George "Soles" King, a former Winterton beachman.

In the days before radio communication the lifeboat had to rely on visual signals and guns. The lightships, seeing a boat in trouble, would use a combination of guns and rockets to summon help from the shore, a different combination being used for each lifeboat area. To alert the Caister boat two guns and two red rockets would be fired every five minutes, the rockets being fired in the direction of the ship in trouble. The lifeboat would, in many cases, have to speak to the lightship to find the location of a wreck, and to be at sea for a period exceeding 24 hours was not unusual.

On New Year's day, 1937, the steamer *Crackshot* went aground in heavy rain on the north Scroby sands. The boat had passed the Cockle lightship close enough to shout a New Year greeting before coming to grief.

"My uncle came and told me that there was a big ship hove to, apparently aground, off Caister. When I went out there was a misty rain and a fresh south-westerly breeze. I rang the bell to call out the crew."

There were plenty of fishermen on the beach at the time, and the pulling and sailing lifeboat *Charles Burton* was soon launched with father Joe Woodhouse as coxswain. A favourable wind ensured they soon reached the Crackshot.

"She was aground on her middle, when the tide fell her back came up and lifted the whole boiler up. She nearly broke her back."

As the ship began to buckle the master gave orders for all the doors to be opened to prevent people being trapped. The only chance was to float the steamer free, and the lifeboatmen and crew set to jettisoning the coal.

"I reckon we got over 300 ton of coal over the side in the time we were there," remembers "Skipper."

Aboard the lifeboat 'Covent Garden'. (Mrs G Haylett)

13th January 1935 and "Skipper" stands with the beach company at their last gathering at the old lookout shed before it was demolished. Many of the men here had only just returned from a 24-hour lifeboat service to the Belgian trawler 'Prosper'. (Ken Jary)

By nightfall five tugs had arrived to help, but they were unable to refloat the 2380 ton ship. Next morning the lifeboat returned to station. A Dutch tug later managed to fit a patch on the hull, and after pumping out some water refloated her. The *Crackshot* was aground on Scroby from Friday until the following Tuesday, and the lifeboat was at sea for 27 hours in their efforts to help with the salvage.

By now the £2 10s investment in the beach company had paid for itself several times over. The salvage money received for the service with the *Crackshot* resulted in a "dole" of £10 per share, with an additional £1 10s for those who had been in the lifeboat, as it was a long service.

Later that year another £2 per share was doled out for a service to the drifter *Cornrigg*, but salvage money was now becoming scarce and most beach companies along the East Coast had been wound up. Caister carried on longer than any other.

In 1935 their lookout and headquarters on the beach had been removed following a dispute with the lord of the manor, a dispute which the company had taken as far as the courts before realising they could not win. An out of court settlement was made, but they lost a building that had served them well for almost 100 years.

The clouds of war had also begun to gather in the late 1930s, and changes were on the way for many people, including the Caister beachmen.

THE MECHANIC

Evening grey and morning red
Will bring down rain upon his head

The onset of the second world war in 1939 saw many local men called up for military service. This brought problems for the beachmen, one of the most serious being a shortage of men available to crew and launch the lifeboat. The *Charles Burton* required a crew of 17 and a shore party of at least 20, and on many occasions at the beginning of the war soldiers billeted in the village and local people not normally connected with the lifeboat were called in to help with launches and sometimes supplement the crew.

The Caister beach company was now the last surviving such group on the East Coast, and the beachmen realised that changing times and conditions meant they could not carry on in their original form for much longer.

A motor lifeboat for the village had first been considered in the 1920s, but the local committee had turned the idea down because they thought it would be too heavy to work off the beach. The RNLI (or the Institution, as it is referred to by beachmen) did not have a successful carriage launched motor lifeboat until the early 1930s, and in 1937 the Caister men had the chance to practise with such a boat.

In 1938 it was decided to station a motor lifeboat at the village and "Skipper," together with his father and another member of the crew, went to Skegness for more trials. These proved satisfactory, and the station was promised a twin screw Liverpool-type boat which was under construction.

Problems arose with the supply of gearboxes for these boats, and as a result Caister was allocated a single engined boat to arrive on station in 1940. The worsening war situation postponed this event, however, and it was not until the next year that it was possible to bring a boat from the Isle of Wight by road, putting it into Yarmouth harbour on May 15, 1941.

The new lifeboat was mounted on a carriage, and a tractor was provided to push it down to the sea, a system that raised doubts in many peoples' minds. But it was a system which had proved successful at other stations. Gone were the days when large groups of men had to expend considerable effort and energy to get their boat into the sea.

Motor lifeboats meant engines to be maintained, and to maintain engines a mechanic was required in the crew. In preparation for the arrival of the new boat this job was advertised in the local Press, and application forms had to be handed to the local secretary. Three Caister men applied. One of them, John Woodhouse, a self taught mechanic,

The 'Jose Neville', the first motor lifeboat to be stationed at Caister.

had to learn by necessity when he bought his first motor fishing boat some years previously.

"I had my own motor boat, that was my experience, and had been in the crew for some years with father as cox. This could have had an influence on it. The main thing was when the district engineer first came down to Caister the war had only been on about a fortnight, and I had my big motor boat on the beach doing a job to the engine. The fishery officer was with me. He was a former mechanic of the Cromer lifeboat, and the district engineer met him and he introduced me to him, do you see, and he see I was the only one with a motor boat on the beach at that time. He said he would see what he could do to see me get the job."

"Skipper" was successful, and went to Aldeburgh for a one week engineering course.

It is necessary here to explain why "Skipper" had not been called up for military service by the time the motor lifeboat arrived. The other members of the old beach company had either already gone into the services or were too old. To put it in his own words: "I registered as a fisherman on 25th May, 1940, the same day we went and rescued the crew from a minesweeper that had been blown up. When we got back to the beach I had a message to meet the district engineer for an appointment for the motor lifeboat. A few days after, a letter came asking me to give two dates when I would be available to go to Norwich for an interview and medical to go into the Patrol Service. I replied and told them I had been appointed mechanic for the Caister lifeboat, and they sent a letter back to say now I was in the service of Trinity Lighthouses afloat would I take this paper to the Superintendent of Trinity to sign. They was all mixed up about the thing so I took it to the

(Left) Mechanic "Skipper" Woodhouse in the early 1960s. (Below) "Skipper" on the left, David on the right, with two Danish sailors and uncle Jack preparing to take stores out to the Danish MTB 'Havoernen' in December 1952.

lifeboat secretary, and he altered it and signed it as hon sec and said I was appointed motor mechanic of the lifeboat, and that was that. Didn't hear any more. Later, all lifeboat crew members liable for call-up got deferment. I got deferment and so did Norford Brown, but everyone else was over military age or already called up."

Throughout the war the lifeboat service came under the control of the Navy and that, according to "Skipper" "was a lot of old trouble." The boats were not called out as frequently as might have been expected, and the majority of launches were to search for planes reported down in the sea. The Caister boat only had one rescue service during the war, and that was for an airman, not ditched from a plane, but who had been bathing on a raft from Scratby beach and drifted out to sea. Many times the lifeboat crew were called to stand by for aircraft returning from bombing raids over Germany, the boat being pulled from the shed on to the beach ready to launch if an unfortunate pilot had to ditch before reaching his base.

After the war things slowly returned to normal, and as the local men came back from the services a regular crew and launching party was again established. The old beach company had been wound up on arrival of the motor lifeboat, and the Caister beachmen were now running a service on similar lines to the many other RNLI stations around the British coastline.

The lifeboat was fitted with a radio telephone in 1949 and "Skipper" had to take an examination for an RT operator's certificate, a qualification he still holds.

The 1950s were to be a busy time for the lifeboat service, and one incident well remembered by Caister men is the grounding of the Danish motor torpedo boat *Havoernen* on the Scroby Sands in thick fog and very heavy seas on December 3, 1952.

The boat had been taking part in a NATO exercise before going aground, and the coastguards sent the Gorleston lifeboat, one of the largest and fastest on the East Coast, to her aid. The Caister beachmen knew the Gorleston boat would not be able to get in close to the stranded vessel because of the shallow water and "Skipper," keeping a close watch on the situation, advised the coxswain, Jimmy Brown, to launch the Caister boat when the tide fell as it was inevitable that they would be needed. Sure enough a message was soon received from the coxswain of the Gorleston boat saying they could not get alongside, and would the Caister boat launch.

At 12.30am the maroons were fired and the *Jose Neville*, with crew members J Brown (coxswain), A Brown (2nd coxswain), J Plummer (bowman), J Woodhouse (mechanic), F King (2nd mechanic), D Woodhouse (3rd mechanic), N Brown, G Codman and the Rev J G Markham, entered the water. Suddenly a large wave struck the boat broadside, causing bowman Plummer to strike his head on the mast, causing an injury that necessitated attention back at the lifeboat station. Other members of the crew, having jumped from the boat, helped the shore crew to haul the boat out of the breakers with the capstan. The tractor, which had become bogged down in the sand, was raised, and at last the lifeboat was launched. The whole operation had taken 1½ hours.

They ran out to the bank and anchored in a deep water channel "Skipper" had discovered the day before when on Scroby looking for drifter pallets to salvage. Three members of the lifeboat crew were able to jump ashore and walk across to the torpedo boat, nine of the Danish crew returning with them to the lifeboat. These men were put aboard a British torpedo boat anchored close by, but before the lifeboat could go in again a helicopter arrived. This was a Naval helicopter which had flown in from Portsmouth, and it proceeded to take off the crew and land them at Yarmouth.

This was the first time a helicopter had been used in conjunction with any lifeboat to rescue the crew of a ship.

The lifeboat went into Yarmouth harbour for the night, returning to the sands the next morning to put a line aboard the Danish boat from an Admiralty salvage ship before returning to her station. Just after midnight the lifeboat was launched again to reconnect the tow which broke during the night. A Danish sailor was brought back to Caister to keep in contact with the ship, using the lifeboat radio. Despite the efforts of the salvage boats, however, the *Havoernen* remained firmly stuck on the sand bank, and as Christmas approached the Mayor of Yarmouth sent out presents and the Caister people organised a collection for the stranded men. "Skipper" was engaged to take out stores and provisions in his fishing boat, and during the next few weeks was to become a regular visitor to the ship and a friend of the Danish crew.

"I had made a study of Norwegian... I read a book and picked up enough words to get by and understand them," he said later.

Six weeks later two Danish tugs and an Admiralty salvage vessel managed to pull the torpedo boat off the sand bank, but this was not the end of the story. To lighten the boat they took off two torpedo warheads and left them on the bank. These had to be recovered, and "Skipper" made an agreement to salvage them for £15. A Danish officer and five seamen went with them.

"When we went there we took a little trolley to pull them across the bank, but they were too heavy and the sand too soft, so we had to take the boat right round the bank to get closer. It took five Danish sailors, me, Weddel and the parson to lift them into our boat." The warheads were taken to a salvage boat waiting nearby.

This was not the longest time a boat had been stranded on Scroby and successfully refloated, for in 1946 a Dutch coaster went aground on February 26 and was not pulled off until April 18.

As mentioned earlier, David had become a fisherman when he left school, and like his brother had always taken a keen interest in the lifeboat. He went out as a crew member at the age of 15 and was the youngest person to go to sea in lifeboat service during the war.

The Woodhouse family also has a claim at the other end of the

The 'Havoernen' on Scroby Sands 1952. (C R Temple)

age range. "Skipper's" uncle went to sea in 1959 at the age of 84, and was still a member of the shore party when he was 87.

As well as being able to turn his hand to the mechanics of an engine "Skipper" was also familiar with much smaller mechanical items, clocks. This skill became useful one day during the war when an enemy bomb landed on the sand dunes near the lifeboat shed and set off 162 land mines. The resultant blast, as well as damaging many houses, blew the clock off the wall of the lifeboat shed, leaving it on the floor in many pieces. These "Skipper" collected together, and after obtaining a new face and glass reassembled the clock from the salvaged pieces. The clock is still working in the shed today.

In February, 1955, a French trawler, the *St Pierre Eglise*, ran aground at Waxham some 12 miles north of Caister. The crew were rescued by the Winterton Lifesaving Company, and the Caister lifeboat was called to the scene three times. The problems were only just starting, however, and it was to be another 55 days before the boat was refloated, an exercise that involved much hard work. After two weeks' fruitless effort Dutch salvage experts were called in, and they in turn employed men from the Caister lifeboat crew, at five shillings an hour, to assist. The Caister men travelled by road to Waxham, and after helping to unload the cargo of fish the following weeks were spent making the ship watertight and clearing away the tons of sand that surrounded her. It was during this work that the Caister men learnt a lot about salvage, and "Skipper" made many friends who were to be useful in the years to come.

The year 1955 was a busy one for the lifeboat, and on August 5 the crew of a small yacht, *Jemima-Puddle-Duck*, were rescued. It was a coincidence that "Skipper" happened to look out of his bedroom window about 4.30am at the very moment a red flare was fired from the direction of the Scroby sands. Seeing the flare, "Skipper" roused the rest of the household and proceeded to the lifeboat shed, from where he phoned the coxswain, Jimmy Brown.

They watched for some minutes, but no more flares were seen. Jimmy then took the glass, and after some searching spotted a small boat on the sands. They decided to launch, and "Skipper" "fired up." The lifeboat was soon at sea. The weather was reasonably fine, fine enough for the local shrimper to be going out, and they proceeded to Scroby. On reaching the bank, where there was only a slight swell, they managed to get the lifeboat within a few yards of the yacht, and the crew of three were able to walk across to them. Two lifeboat men went to look at the yacht, but found it was holed, so the lifeboat made its way back to the village and landed the crew on the beach about 7am. The three men were taken to the Woodhouse cottage for some hot tea while they awaited transport to take them to the Sailors' Home at Yarmouth. By 7.30am the sea conditions began to deteriorate, the wind having freshened, and the shrimpers were running for the shore.

It later transpired that the yacht had gone aground some time before midnight and had burnt all but one of their flares trying to raise the alarm. One passing ship had signalled them with a Morse lamp and

The French trawler 'St Pierre Eglise' on Waxham beach where she was stranded for 55 days. The Caister beachmen travelled by road each day to assist with the salvage operation.

they thought help would then be on its way, but for some unexplained reason the ship had not reported the incident. By 4.30am they realised what had happened and fired their last flare, the flare "Skipper" had seen. In all probability the heavy swell that developed during the morning would have overwhelmed the yacht, and the crew drowned.

This incident happened during the height of the holiday season, and at that time many people camped on the dunes near the lifeboat shed. In his eagerness to get to the shed in response to the maroons one of the crew tripped over the ropes, bringing down tents on screaming children, and annoyed adults and caused complete confusion among the campers who thought they were being attacked.

About a month later, on a day with a fresh wind blowing from the west, "Skipper" had finished tripping when some schoolchildren pointed out something in the water off the holiday camp. Running to the shed, and looking through the glass, "Skipper" could see a small dinghy floating out to sea with three people in it, one frantically waving for help. He fired the maroons and phoned the coastguards to say the

The London collier 'Harfry' aground off Hemsby in June 1955. The Caister lifeboat, which can be seen alongside, stood by for two days before the ship was refloated by tugs.

The 'Royal Thames' (1964-1969), the last RNLI lifeboat to be stationed at Caister.

Caister boat was about to launch. The 2nd cox, "Mabby" Brown took charge, and within seven minutes of the telephone call they were at sea, making radio contact with Yarmouth coastguards.

The small plane from the local airfield, used to take pleasure flights, joined the lifeboat in the search and soon the dinghy was located, still drifting out to sea and heading for rough water. It was a metal dinghy used by campers, not designed for going far out to sea and with no ballast tanks. "Skipper" described it as "a tin bath." The boys in the dinghy, one aged 14, one 15 and one 16, were by now in a bad way, the eldest having given up hope of rescue and convinced he was about to die. They were taken aboard, as was the "tin bath," and taken back to the beach to recover.

In the 1960s it became apparent that a twin engined boat was needed to replace the *Jose Neville*. The engine had become a problem. Not only were replacement parts difficult to obtain, but the engines in all these types of boats were unreliable, causing the Institution much concern. In 1964 Caister was allocated one of the new twin engined boats of the Oakley design, and "Skipper" found himself in Cowes for a four-week course to become familiar with the new engines. As a regular crew member, "Skipper" was entitled to a small wage, or retaining fee, from the RNLI which started at £2 per week rising over the years to £12. Not a great wage, but as he has since said, "it helped to keep the wolves from the door."

The new boat was named the *Royal Thames*, but unbeknown at the time it was to have only a short service at Caister.

"SKIPPER" JACK

Skipper on watch.(Paul Durrant)

Until 1947 the method of calling the crew together for a launch was the sound of the call-out bell, a large bell at the rear of the lifeboat shed. A westerly wind could easily drown the sound, and so a call-out man was needed, as described earlier. The bell was replaced by maroons, and while in many places these were the responsibility of the local coastguard, at Caister the lifeboatmen usually fired them.

The Woodhouse family lived close to the beach and a member of the family was nearly always available. Therefore, the job of firing the maroons often fell upon them. It was an accepted system that the coastguards would phone the coxswain who in turn would phone "Skipper" to fire the maroons. In recent years new methods have been introduced to summon a crew, but "Skipper" is confident it is the sound of the maroons which reassure the crews of vessels in trouble and keep them calm, knowing the lifeboat is on its way. And he quotes the example of August, 1985, when a young man was about to try and swim ashore from a dinghy when he heard the Caister maroon. If he had left his dinghy he would probably have drowned, as he could not swim. But knowing that help was on its way he stayed put and was rescued.

The more modern method adopted by many stations of personal bleepers is, in "Skipper's" personal opinion, not satisfactory. It should be stated, however, that for many stations, particularly where the crew are employed away from the station, the personal call system has many advantages and is today widely used. The Caister station still uses traditional maroons.

THE BEACHCOMBER

The nearer the Burr the farther the storm
The farther the Burr the nearer the storm

Fishing, salvage and lifeboats have been an interwoven thread in the lives of seaside communities for generations past, and it has been seen from earlier chapters how a beachman like "Skipper" occupied much of his time. But the financial reward received for lifeboat service alone was not enough to make a living, and the main income had to come from other sources, one of which was beachcombing.

An easterly wind meant that the beachmen would be continually patrolling the beach, be it day or night, to keep a lookout for anything of interest being washed up. The local name given to this activity of beachcombing was "porking" or "scouring," the latter being used when looking for money or other small objects and the beach was being examined in greater detail. Small pieces of amber were often found, but the most common finds were coal or wood. The wood was collected over the year and stored. When there was enough it was sold to local farmers for building barns and outbuildings, or if not suitable for this was disposed of as firewood. Salvage obtained in this way was an important income for many people.

There are no known - or perhaps it should be said, admitted - instances of smuggling activities on Caister beach within living memory, although it is not unreasonable to assume that such practices have taken place in years gone by.

In 1800 a public footpath running from the main Ormesby road to the beach was ordered to be stopped up. The reasons given by the authorities were that "these ways are frequently used by evil disposed persons to commit depredations on the several lands and premises thereto adjoining, but more especially for a more easy access to the sea side for the purpose of plunder."

It can be assumed from this statement that smuggling was a problem in the 18th century.

There have, however, been many cases where cargo has been washed ashore, and before the custom officers have been alerted an undisclosed amount has found its way off the beach and been spirited away. The true beachmen, however, claim not to have been party to such deals, and although the temptation has sometimes been great they have always tried to make money from such goods honestly, by receiving the true salvage payments. In many instances this proved a problem, as the percentage of value offered by the customs men was often considered too little. The beachmen would then proceed to argue their case, hoping to eventually reach an agreement. In 1955 such an argument ended with the beachmen threatening to take the Receiver of Wrecks to court for wrongfully dealing with wrecked property.

During the war years a great variety of goods were washed up on the beach from ships that had been destroyed, sometimes many miles away. Some of these items could, with a little ingenuity, be reclaimed for use, particularly during these lean times. Butter and lard, even if washed up in damaged containers, could be melted down so that the stones and sand sank to the bottom, leaving a useful layer that could be taken off the top; flour, even if packed in sacks, could be cut open and the clean, dry contents recovered from the middle of the sack where the water had not penetrated. Wood had many uses and could be stockpiled for the future while cigarettes, although soaked by sea water, could produce a reasonable supply of tobacco once dried by the fire.

Many of these items would be considered beyond salvage by the customs, but the beachmen could find a use for almost anything.

Among the more unusual items washed up on Caister beach from time to time have been bales of cotton (too big and heavy), crates of matches (millions of wet matches are of no use to anyone) and barrels of raspberry pulp (there was always a sale for a good empty barrel, although in this instance the customs paid 50s (£2.50) salvage for the full barrel).

Sometimes the memory of a beachcombing adventure brings back a smile to "Skipper's" face. "I was on the beach with an old man from California and we found an old ship's timber, a big bit with a curve in it, awkward to carry. He said, look, I can get two shillings for this off an old farmer if we take it to California. We were then about a quarter a mile south of Cali, so I said when we get about half way along we'll lay it down and have a rest. When we go to pick it up we had the deuce of a job to get it up. We first got it on one shoulder then the other, but after a long struggle we got it up. We both had it on a shoulder, but when we looked up we were facing each other. I say, well, you're nearest California, walk you backwards. Anyway, I managed to turn around. Old Sugars was about 70."

The collection of driftwood from the beaches was an occupation that had been carried out by beachmen for centuries. In 1724 Daniel Defoe had noticed, as he made his tour of Britain, that at Winterton most of the barns, sheds, stables and the like were built of old planks, beams and timbers from wrecked ships. Through the 18th and 19th centuries the supply of timber from wrecks was abundant enough to allow nearly all coastal buildings to be so constructed.

The week before Christmas, 1948, is still remembered by many people along the Norfolk coastline, and particularly in the Caister area. The motor-ship *Bosphorus*, bound for Hull, grounded on Happisburgh Sands and had to jettison her cargo of oranges, worth several thousands of pounds. These oranges, one of the first shipments to reach this country after the war, were intended for a Christmas allocation to the north of England. A north-east wind guaranteed that the cargo would eventually arrive on the beach, and the beachmen were ready.

Oranges galore — the beach covered with oranges just before Christmas 1948 after the 'Bosphorus' ran aground on the Haisboro' Sands.

"We set the alarm clock and was up about three," "Skipper" remembers. "We had rugged our boat out for shrimping the day before, and had the bath tins and that all in her. I rug up a light and me and David and my father filled up the bath tins with oranges and took them back to the shed."

By daylight the beach was covered with oranges and the local population, eager to obtain some of the scarce fruit for Christmas, were soon there. Children were given time off from school to go to the beach, and soon the fruit had been cleared. Many people came from the inland villages by bicycle or any means of transport they could find as the good news spread. Some hours later people were still arriving to search in vain for the fruit, and the local policeman directed them to the lifeboat shed. "Here we was a selling of 'em nine for a shilling (5p)," recalls "Skipper."

The large canvas buoys used by the drifters, called "palletts" were another item worth salvaging, either picked up on the beach or from the Scroby sandbank. "Skipper" often took his boat out in search of these, because "we got a good customer for them, an old Scotsman, Christmas Charlie, he used to treat us pretty well for them." Taking naturalists out to the Scroby Sands was another regular pursuit for "Skipper" and David. "I was the first one to find the grey seals with pups on Scroby." These seals have now been replaced by the common seal, but some years ago the grey seal was numerous and many people were ferried out to see them.

One activity that was and still is a useful pocket money earner for beachmen is the collection of cuttlefish. The shells from these fish are

"SKIPPER" JACK

washed up in cold weather, collected and then washed in fresh water before being dried and left to bleach in the sun. "Skipper" at one time advertised these in the Cage Bird magazine, but the trade was killed by the railway when carriage became too expensive. The best price he could expect to receive was £1 per stone. They are, however, still collected when the opportunity arises, although only in small amounts.

Taking holidaymakers out for sea trips was an important summer occupation for many beachmen going back to the 1920s. "Skipper's" first motor boat, the *Endeavour*, was primarily used for "tripping," along with several other boats from the Caister beach. The success of tripping depended on the weather, and in the years following the war it was not unusual for each boat to make up to 14 trips a day, each trip lasting about 45 minutes. This was during the years when holidaymakers did not seek such diverse entertainment as they do today, and a trip out in a small boat was one of the highlights of a seaside holiday.

In 1960 "Skipper" had a new boat built, the *Seabird*, and this was also used for tripping. But by the 1980s holidaymakers wanted something more exciting and the boat was sold in 1987, ending the tradition of sea trips from Caister beach.

Another stretch of sand well-known to "Skipper" is the island of Scroby, lying some two miles from the mainland. This he has visited for many different reasons over the years - salvage, lifesaving, tripping or just to visit when taking local naturalists out to study the wildlife.

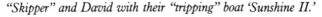

"Skipper" and David with their "tripping" boat 'Sunshine II.'

As the 'Sunshine' puts to sea the house flag can be seen at the mast head, the red, white and blue squares signalling the letter W.

To the present day holidaymaker the sands appear as a golden line rising out of the North Sea like some romantic South Sea island. They have, over the years had a colourful history. As far back as the 16th century Scroby was in the news when a bailiff of Great Yarmouth decided it would be fitting to claim the island, then about a mile long and with vegetation growing on it, for the town. Accompanied by other town officials he put to sea and landed on the sand, naming it Yarmouth Island and declaring it to be part of the borough. A hedge was erected to encourage the sands to accumulate, and after a dinner toasts were drunk and a game of bowls played before the party returned to the mainland.

Sir Edward Clere, Lord of the Manor of Scratby, promptly denounced the whole thing illegal and claimed the island was part of his manor. He took possession and erected a timber house on Scroby as part of his claim.

Many people from the town were by now making excursions out to Scroby to see the wildlife as well as "feasting, playing bowls and other pastimes." The goods of shipwrecked vessels were washed ashore there, and in 1582 it was reported "sundry silks, wax and such like rich commodities" were found. By the end of the century, however a severe storm resulted in the sands being reclaimed by the sea, so ending all disputes of ownership.

In 1917 the sandbank again appeared above the sea at all tides although the East Coast floods of 1953 again reduced it almost to sea level. Since then the sands have reformed and in 1957 attempts were

Happy holidaymakers return after a trip to Scroby in 1938.

made to plant marram grass but this proved unsuccessful.

Over the years many ships have come to grief here and until quite recently the masts sticking out of the sand acted as a grim reminder of those unfortunate not to get off again. The standing of the Danish gunboat *Havoernen* has already been mentioned and among many other victims of the sands have been the brigantine *Briton* in 1825, the collier brig *Amelia* in 1857, the schooner *Dart* in 1915 and the Belgian trawler *Yarmouth* in 1950. Ships of all types and sizes have run into the sands in fog and storm despite the lights and buoys that mark its presence.

Wildlife has found a home on this bleak island, in 1947 terns first nested there in varying degrees of success, both the Common tern and the Sandwich tern. The Common Seal and the Grey Seal have also lived on Scroby, sometimes to the annoyance of local inshore fishermen but to the delight of naturalists. The Grey Seal or Atlantic Seal was first recorded there in 1958 and Skipper can claim to be one of the first to notice it and although it was then thought the late autumn weather would be too rough for them to breed, pups were seen in the December.

This natural breakwater shelters the beaches of Yarmouth and Caister from the force of the seas rolling across the North Sea and to beachmen like Skipper, Scroby Sands are as well known as the local beach. Over the years the island has provided much work for the lifeboats and at one time was described as 'Treasure Island' because of the valuable salvage it produced.

(Left and previous page) The 'Luna', wrecked on Caister Beach in 1980. A twentieth century wreck more reminiscent of the early nineteenth century. (Poppyland Photos)

The days of wrecked sailing ships littering Caister beach were recalled in October 1980 when the 77 year old brigantine *Luna*, which had earlier developed engine trouble on a voyage to Holland, was driven ashore onto the beach in gale force winds and quickly broke up. The Gorleston lifeboat ran aground in the shallow water as she tried to reach the stricken vessel and Caister lifeboat was launched. A big swell sent the *Shirley Jean Adye* crashing into its launching trailer, tearing a hole in the stern of the boat, but the Caister men pressed on undaunted. The drama of the launch was only completely appreciated when the boat returned to station and the hull could be properly examined.

The family who owned the boat had managed to scramble to the beach in the darkness and, sad to say, less scrulpulous beachcombers were on the scene robbing the wreckage, even as the survivors sought to salvage their storm-battered possessions from what had been their home.

A more positive note was sounded by "Skipper" and the Caister lifeboat team. The hostel in Yarmouth was unable to offer accommodation to the shipwrecked family, and a decision was made to ensure that in future hospitality could be offered in Caister. The consequence was that several months later two renovated cottages were opened by the Caister Volunteer Rescue Service should such a need arise again.

THE FISHERMAN

Red sky at night is the sailor's delight
Red sky in the morning is the sailor's warning.

Longshoremen in their small boats have worked with lines, nets and pots to catch a great variety of fish for home consumption and financial gain for many years. The fishermen have experienced good times and hard times - the supply of fish fluctuating - and these irregular rewards have become part of life.

Every coastal fishing community in the British Isles has different traditions and techniques unique to that area.

It has been seen in an earlier chapter how shrimping was one of "Skipper's" first exploits into fishing, and shrimps were to be an important catch for many years to come. During the spring months both push and pull nets were employed.

"We used to have a method of fishing in a low. There was a big deep low along between the Camp and the north piles (the beach at the northern end of the village), and I had a bow net fixed up on lines, and I used to take a dog with me, and got the dog to swim across the low to get connection. Used to get a couple of boys on the beach, and I was on the bank. We used to pull it along like that."

Another method, using the boat to catch pink shrimps, was to let the boat lay broadside and drift the net along, using a sea anchor, or drogue, to help pull the net with the tide, as the tide is stronger at the top than at the bottom.

Some of the shrimps were sold to merchants. The majority were boiled at home and sold locally, the whole family being involved with either taking orders or helping to walk round the village knocking on doors.

"If we had been out every day of the week shrimping I reckon we would tramp a hundred miles round the village selling them," he recalls. A good day's shrimping could produce eight pecks, a measure still in use today where shrimps are sold in pints and pecks. A peck is a dry measure of two gallons.

Two types of shrimp are caught off this part of the coast, pink and brown. Pink shrimps lay away from the beach on rough ground, living on worms in the sand, while brown shrimps live on the sands close to the beach. Today, pink shrimps have all but disappeared off Caister beach, the theory being that detergents and other pollutants in the sea have killed the worms the shrimps once thrived on.

"Shrimping would have been one of the main things. I got my first boat in 1929, but we didn't do a lot of fishing the first year, used to take anglers off. Then we fitted her up with sails to go herring fishing. We got the sails out of my father's old boat called the *Seek and Find* - we done all sorts with her, herring catching, shrimping, trawling, long lining."

Caister has never been well-known for inshore fishing, the shallow waters and sand banks limiting the quantity of fish. If there had been more profitable inshore fishing not so many of the local men would have turned to the drifter fishing from Yarmouth. "Skipper" and David, however, have perservered with inshore work and have succeeded by using a combination of experience and skill to make reasonable catches.

There are many different methods used by inshore fishermen. One used for many years has been long lining. This type of fishing appears to be a method that had died out for some years at Caister. It had been popular before the first world war, and in the early 1930s heaps of discarded lines still lay around in the sheds.

"Skipper" and his uncle decided to revive the method to catch skate, or roker as they have always been known among local fishermen. They managed to obtain some second hand hemp lines that had become unsuitable for a larger type of boat where a winch was used to haul them.

"We sent away and got some hooks and rugged them up. I reckon we revived something that hadn't been done about here for years."

The fishing village of Caister c1900. On the left can be seen one of the many net chambers where nets were repaired and tanned for the fishermen.

A sting-ray caught off Caister in 1954. The beachmen would take the liver from the fish and boil it, the resulting mixture being a recognised embrocation for lumbago and rheumatism.

A long line had 300 hooks attached, later extended to 600, the maximum two people could handle. Before setting off each hook had to be baited. It was a job that could take up to 1½ hours. Before the hooks could be baited, however, the bait had to be caught.

"We used to go out and catch the herring on the high water, and we'd come home, if the wind was favourable we'd sail or else we had to row. After a bit of grub we'd bait up and then sail down to Hemsby Hole, a nice lot of rooker laid there, and then we laid the hooks."

This operation of first catching the bait and then the fish could take from early morning until dusk, or later, depending on the state of the tides. The obvious question to ask is why the bait was not caught one day and the lining done the next. "Skipper's" answer to this is: "Tomorrow never comes, 300 hooks in the sea is the same as a bird in the hand is worth two in the bush, if you're lucky you can go again the next day." A fine example of how the beachmen would not miss an opportunity, hard work being the last consideration.

This technique of long lining involves laying lines with the hooks attached about every seven feet on three foot long "snoods," or strings. The lines, after being baited, are laid in tin baths, each layer covered with marram grass to keep them separate. When the fishing ground is reached the hooks are shot over the side with a stick while the boat is either rowed or motored slowly along. Every 40 hooks a small 3lb anchor is attached. After a period of about two hours the line is hauled in, and as the fish come to the top of the water they are lifted out.

"SKIPPER" JACK

Skipper the fisherman. (Paul Durrant)

This fishing occupied the autumn months, sometimes lasting up until Christmas. The fish were sent to Lowestoft market, sometimes being taken by the local fishmonger, "Starchy" Mann, who went daily to get supplies for his shop.

Drift netting is a system where the net is kept upright in the water by corks and leads and allowed to drift at right angles to the flow of the tide. One end is fixed to the boat and the other end attached to a floating buoy. If the net should drift more rapidly than the boat, tangling can occur. With this method of fishing both boat and net are at the mercy of wind and tide. By this method the inshore fisherman catches herring, but this has declined over the years. Gone are the days when the fisherman was in danger of overloading his boat because fish were so plentiful, or so abundant they could sometimes be lifted from the water by the oars of the boat.

Many small boats have sailed from Caister beach in search of herring over the years, and as with other fish the amounts they have caught have fluctuated greatly. In the heyday of the Yarmouth herring fishing the small boats would not have much luck until after the drifters had returned home towards the end of October, the reason being that when the drifters landed big catches many herring would be dropped into the river at the fishwharf. They drifted out to sea and kept the longshore herring away. Today, when there are no drifters working from nearby ports, local longshoremen can expect to catch their fish through to Christmas.

The fishing grounds off this part of the coast are not suitable for shellfish, but in the early 1950s several boats tried their hand at catching crab. Pots were laid and reasonable catches made, but the work involved was not really justified by the final result. The crabs were never top quality.

"Skipper" and David boiled their crabs in the coppers used for shrimps, but eventually the crabs gave way to other fishing.

It has been mentioned that "Skipper" had a motor boat built in 1934, and this larger boat was used for mackerel fishing until just before the war started. A trip to catch mackerel would involve shooting 27 nets.

Sea trout (Salmo Trutta), a close relation of the salmon, is a "top of the market" fish and a valuable catch for the inshore fisherman. Similar in habit to the salmon, the sea trout spends part of its life in freshwater for the breeding season, and the remainder at sea where it feeds.

"Skipper's" grandfather fished from Caister beach for trout from the turn of the century, and "Skipper" recalls that when he first started this type of fishing "the nets we used hadn't changed since Bible times, they were just a simple net." This was soon to change, however, and "Skipper" was the first fisherman to try putting a "poke," or cod-end, in the trout net.

"First year I got this poke to work we were getting a nice lot of fish, and other people weren't getting nowhere so many as us. They used to come back and talk about the fish they would lose rather than the fish they would get." The addition of the "poke" revolutionised the trout fishing. "One crew went on strike till he got me to put a poke in his net," "Skipper" recalls.

Skipper preparing his nets.

Tractors have replaced manpower to launch the inshore fishing boats and "Skipper" now finds this an essential item in his work. (Bill Crowe)

During the war years the beachmen concentrated on fishing all year round as there were no holidaymakers for summer tripping. Although the regulations banned fishing during the hours of darkness this was usually the best time to make a catch, and "Skipper" and David recall that they were often back on the beach at daybreak, having completed their work before they were supposed to have even started. It was difficult to find a market to begin with, the traditional fish markets having closed. Many fishermen thought all fishing was finished until the war came to an end, but "Skipper" persevered.

On the first trip of the war years they caught 4 stone of trout. With no market to send it to they rowed home and looked in the telephone directory and picked out Mac Fisheries of Norwich. The firm agreed to take the catch and instructed them to wrap each fish in newspaper and then wrap the whole lot in damp sacks, and send them to Norwich as soon as possible. Sacks were obtainable with a little persuasion from the soldiers, even if it meant a few less sandbags, and all that was left for "Skipper" to do was to walk down to the nearest bus stop and put the parcel in the care of Eastern Counties Omnibus Company, which no doubt kept it away from the other passengers on that journey.

This system worked, and soon other fishermen who had hung up their nets for the duration of the war were out again following his example. This carried on until 1945.

One day in 1942 a German airman, who had swum ashore from his ditched plane, safely landed on the shore only to get caught up in the barbed wire at the top of the beach. Seeing "Skipper" just off the beach he began to shout and wave, believing they were his colleagues in their rubber dinghy. Unknown to him the remaining members of his crew had been picked up by the Home Guard at Hemsby, but the noise he made aroused the local Home Guard who took a little time to realise that "Skipper's" boat was not another German crew trying to get ashore. "We made a good catch that day," he remembers. "By the time he had finished hollerin' we were far enough out to shoot, and in the first haul we had one fish weighing 19¼lb."

Mines posed a problem for local fishermen, but "Skipper" kept a close watch when any were laid and, knowing the beach and tides, was able to advise both fishermen and patrolling soldiers where danger lay. The mines were laid only just below the surface of the beach, and after a good blow or scour many would be exposed, necessitating the attention of bomb disposal teams from the Yarmouth Naval base.

As most beaches were out of bounds to everybody the system of "draw netting" was difficult if not impossible for most fishermen. Draw netting involved one man on the beach to anchor one end of the net while the boat was rowed round in a circle, paying out the net, until the other end was on the beach as well. The net could now be pulled in, a task that took time and a considerable amount of effort. Not only could there be two stone of fish in the net, which in itself would not pose any problems, but when this was added to the weed, tide and swell, it was a method of fishing that was very hard. It was sometimes made more precarious when a mine was dragged up in the net as well.

July 1982. Skipper sets off on a fishing trip. (Paul Durrant)

"SKIPPER" JACK

To try and find an alternative, "Skipper" approached the fishery officer to find out other methods that would not entail them coming ashore. For reasons unknown the officer refused to divulge any details. It was not until the war had finished that "Skipper" found out from "Downtide" West, of Sheringham, how they fished with flax nets, using the drifting method. Flax nets were obtained, and for several years they were successful until a fall in the catches made the men look at other different methods.

In the 1970s a new mono-filament net was tried with varying degrees of success, and this has now become the standard net, used by all local inshore fishermen. One advantage is that fish can now be caught during the day, the nets being almost invisible in the water. "Skipper" agrees that today's fishing is vastly improved from the systems used only a few years ago. But the catches of sea trout are again on the decline, probably due to the improvement in net design causing over-fishing.

Since 1952 it has been necessary to obtain an annual licence to catch trout, and the season runs from April 1 until October 1. Before the mid-1960s the season was from March until September 1, and "Skipper" remembers the year when he cast his net near the Manor House Hotel, a good customer.

"We got one in the first draw of 10lb. I ran up the steps to the hotel and put it on the scales, still alive. The manageress said she would give us 1s 6d a pound, and could we bring another 14lb the next morning? So the next day I took another 14lb. Oh yes, she said. Fourteen pounds, 14 shillings. Why pay less today, I said. Well, she replied, they went out of season at midnight."

There was not a large market in the village for the trout beside the hotel, although sometimes the rector or the coastguard commander would buy one. "But you had to put the price up afore you went, to allow them to knock it down again," said "Skipper."

The craft of making a net by hand is known as braiding, and although today a lot of the nets used are factory made, many prefer a handmade net designed for their own particular purpose. "Skipper" has braided nets for himself and others for many years. It is a skill he has passed on to local fishermen, although those who can make a net today can be counted on one hand.

The process of hand braiding demands very little in the way of equipment, but it does require considerable dexterity and patience. Techniques vary considerably in different parts of the country. "Skipper" has in the past designed and made nets to suit a variety of local conditions, and today is still in demand as a net maker.

Many fishing communities are now diminishing, the fishermen's cottages being renovated to become holiday homes. Access to the beach is being restricted. The land once used for drying nets and mending and storing boats has become valuable building land or car parking areas. Large trawlers, mainly foreign, work closer inshore and destroy the traditional fishing grounds of the inshore fisherman.

*This group of four pictures
shows "Skipper" Woodhouse at
work as a fisherman.*

"SKIPPER" JACK

At Caister, the boats traditionally kept on the open beach just above the high water mark are now moved to the shelter of the sand dunes. This has reduced vandalism and saves the need to move the boats when a storm blows up.

Today's fisherman relies on a tractor and trailer as part of his equipment to get the boat over the dunes to the sea, a system that has also reduced the effort needed to launch. There are now only a handful of full-time fishermen working from the beach. The majority are part time, and during the past few years this number has increased as more people try to reap an income from the sea. Many of the new breed of fishermen, however, lack the experience needed, and find the work not so rewarding and easy as it might appear.

Traditions take a long time to die, but in many places the old ways have gone, never to return. But the inshore fisherman is still a man of rugged character with a determination to pit himself against nature, sometimes in conditions in which many people would not even venture out.

"Skipper" recalls the night in May, 1938: "One of the worst nights ever, no sign of bad weather when suddenly a gale springs up. We managed to haul, and motored south only to be met by the Gorleston lifeboat who thought we were going to try and make it into the harbour, but we told him we were making for Caister beach. The Cromer lifeboat was also out that night and towed in a fishing boat that had blown helplessly out to sea."

A VOLUNTEER

Evening red and morning grey
Will send the traveller on his way.

Towards the end of the 1960s the RNLI began a review of all lifeboat stations with the aim of rationalising the organisation. The results of this review included the planned closure of several stations, of which Caister was to be one.

The first indications the Caister men had of this decision was during an exercise in March, 1969, when an RNLI official told them their station was on the review list. "We thought the best thing to do was to prepare for the worst and hope for the best, and so we made preparations of what to do if the station closed," "Skipper" remembers. The beachmen planned how they could start up with a private boat if necessary, hopeful that when the RNLI heard of their plans they might change their minds and keep the station open.

"We knew little or nothing about the boat going," said "Skipper." "The coxswain, the secretary, and the parson (who was chairman) went to London for a meeting with the RNLI, and the cox came back and said they didn't know exactly what was going to happen." Unknown to the local men, however, the decision had been made. A few days later the local Press was knocking on "Skipper's" cottage door at breakfast time to tell him the closure announcement was to be made that day. One lifeboatman, Jimmy Brown, heard the news on the local radio as he was having breakfast. Not a good start to his day.

"Skipper" carries on the story. "We was going pleasure tripping that morning... newspaper people came down photographing and wanted me to open the doors of the lifeboat shed so they could take some pictures." " Skipper" would not accept the news from the reporters, and told them, "The station won't close, if they take away this one we'll run one of our own." By lunchtime the local secretary was able to confirm the reports, and the beachmen's worst fears were realised.

This was July 14, 1969, and the boat was due to leave the station the following October. Coxswain Jack Plummer, who had been due to retire from the service in the July, was granted an extension of service to cover the remaining few weeks.

The arguments for keeping a lifeboat stationed at Caister were based on the opinion that there was a need for a shallow draft boat capable of reaching ships stranded on the North Scroby and other sandbanks to the north of Yarmouth. The Gorleston boat, although fast, could not work in some of these shallow waters. But this was an argument the RNLI did not agree with. There were, however, several groups who supported the station, one of these being the inshore fishermen of Great Yarmouth, who unsuccessfully petitioned the Queen for help. RNLI officials came to Caister, and a public meeting was held where they explained their case for closure and offered a rubber inshore boat as a replacement. This was overwhelmingly rejected by those present. A 10-man committee was established to look into the possibilities and problems of establishing a private volunteer lifeboat station.

A privately owned lifeboat was not a new idea on this coast. Indeed, in the early years of the service there were many. The Sheringham lifeboat, the *Augusta*, was built in 1836 at the instigation of a local family, the Upchers, and given to the fishermen of the village for their protection. In 1894 a replacement was built, the *Henry Ramey Upcher*, and this again was operated by the local fishermen until 1935 - despite the fact that the RNLI had a lifeboat stationed at Sheringham from 1867.

A few miles from Caister, at the small community of California, a lifeboat service was maintained by the local beachmen from 1854 until 1894 with a boat called *Prince Albert*. When the beach company ceased to operate, this boat went to the Essex town of Walton-on-the-Naze where a disagreement had led to a privately run lifeboat being established in opposition to the RNLI. The boat was renamed the *True-to-the-Core*. One of the early Caister lifeboats, the *Godsend*, which saved more than 400 lives during her 25 years' service at the village, was sold by the RNLI in 1892 and from 1901 until 1907 was in service as the Frinton volunteer lifeboat, the *Sailors' Friend*.

The Caister beachmen, with a retired lieutenant from the Dutch Air Force acting as chairman, set about the difficult task of re-establishing a lifeboat station at the village. Help and advice came from near and far, including Boulmer in Northumberland where a private service had been set up some months previously. Even if resources were limited, there was a great determination to try to maintain the long tradition of life saving the station had established.

Caister was perhaps lucky and had some advantages over other stations who might have considered such a move. The RNLI agreed to leave the launching carriage, a major part of the necessary equipment, and Great Yarmouth council agreed to let the building at a peppercorn rent. These two items were crucial to any plans to replace the lifeboat, and although there was a lot of opposition from many members of the public there was enough support to give the beachmen encouragement to carry on.

The morning of October 17, 1969 arrived, the day the *Royal Thames* was due to leave the station for the last time. "We'd been herring fishing that night, didn't get done till the early hours of the morning," said "Skipper." "Time I'd had breakfast and got done was time to go across to the shed and launch the lifeboat. We got home by dinner and went fishing again that afternoon." The crew had taken the boat to the Oulton Broad yard of Fletchers, where it stayed for several months for a complete refit before being restored to RNLI service.

One of the first tasks now facing the beachmen was to raise a crew, and a meeting was held in the lifeboat shed to ascertain how many men were available and willing. The RNLI coxswain, Jack Plummer, had retired from the service, and several other members of the old crew had decided for various reasons that they would not become involved with another lifeboat. There was, however, still enough interest among the remainder. Several new faces also turned up at the meeting, where a new coxswain, "Mabby" Brown, was elected with Benny Read as second cox. "Skipper" Woodhouse was elected mechanic. The next obstacle to overcome was the availability of a boat.

"Skipper" offered the new service the use of his 16ft fibre glass dinghy, complete with outboard engine, to maintain a service until a more substantial boat could be obtained, and the following Saturday this was placed in the now empty shed. Rope, and the myriad of other equipment needed if the boat was to be used for life saving work, was begged or borrowed and stored in an old tin chest rescued from the November bonfire. The gear was completed by the inclusion of a bottle of home-made parsnip wine. The coastguards were informed that Caister had a boat ready for service, and the Volunteer Rescue Service was in business.

In November, a public meeting decided to launch an appeal for £50,000 to buy a new boat, but this met with little success, and before much money had been collected the firm which was to have built the boat went into liquidation. The beachmen carried on, however, and in March, 1970, the small dinghy went to the assistance of a Dutch motor coaster, the *Interwave*, which had grounded on Scroby Sands. The crew had been taken off earlier by the Gorleston lifeboat, and the Lloyd's agent asked Caister to take two crew members back to the ship where a Dutch tug was trying to salvage her. The lifeboat crew of three consisted of coxswain "Mabby" Brown, Benny Read, and "Skipper" Woodhouse.

Children at the local senior school, whose headmaster had himself been a member of the RNLI crew, held a sponsored walk and raised enough money to buy and equip an inflatable inshore rescue boat, and it was with this that the new service saved its first life, rescuing the occupant of an overturned Enterprise sailing dinghy.

Early in 1973 enquiries revealed that there were secondhand lifeboats for sale in North Norfolk ports, where they were in use as fishing boats, and on "Skipper's" recommendation the Caister men decided to look at one at Wells. The asking price was £4200, but after some bargaining £200 was knocked off providing they paid within six months. A deposit was paid and the boat was their's, the agreement being signed while they sailed out of the river at Wells.

The date was April 5, 1973, and the boat was brought home to be put on the carriage the RNLI had left at the station. A bulldozer was borrowed to pull the new boat into the shed, and at last Caister had a replacement lifeboat. Even if it was a fishing boat.

"SKIPPER" JACK

The new volunteer lifeboat 'Shirley Jean Adye' is launched on August 5th 1973. (C R Temple)

The boat had been built in 1952 and used by the RNLI at St Abbs in Scotland as the *W Ross MacArthur of Glasgow*. From 1963 until 1969 she was in the reserve fleet, and then bought by Mr Case of Wells and used for fishing.

After four months of hard work the boat was in a condition that satisfied the coxswain and the crew, and on Sunday, August 5, 1973, it was officially launched from Caister beach and named *Shirley Jean Adye*. The dreams and hopes of the beachmen were at last a reality. Caister could again go "on station" with a full size lifeboat.

The new boat had only been in service only a short time when a serious illness meant "Skipper" had to relinquish his position as regular mechanic early in 1975. This ended an active lifeboat career of over 40 years, but with the true determination of these tough men "Skipper," after a few months' recuperation, was back with the lifeboatmen, although he was not able to take up his previous position. There was still plenty of work for him to become involved with, however, and his experience was to prove invaluable in the months ahead.

January 12, 1978, was to be a memorable day for the Volunteer Rescue Service. At 2am Gorleston coastguards received a Mayday call from a Greek ship, *Sea Diamond*, then south-east of Lowestoft. The Lowestoft and Gorleston lifeboats were launched in a storm where the wind reached gusts of over 80mph and the waves were so high that searching by radar was impossible and parachute flares were blown away. The engines of the Gorleston boat stopped, and the Lowestoft boat left the search area to go to her assistance. All RNLI lifeboats further north were unable to launch because of storm damage, and the only boat left for the coastguards to call on was Caister. But with such heavy seas running it was doubtful if a beach launching was possible.

Coxswain Brown was called and the maroons fired to summon the crew, who were then told of the situation. After a quick discussion they decided to launch if at all possible, and the boat was brought out of the shed on to the storm swept beach. After two hours toil, which entailed towing the boat about 2½ miles along the beach to where there was smoother water, the Caister boat was at last launched and began to make its way south, much to the surprise of the coastguards. The Gorleston lifeboat had managed to get its engines running again, and now three lifeboats were able to search for the stricken ship with the assistance of a helicopter which was able to direct them to wreckage it had spotted.

The Caister boat recovered a body from the sea when the helicopter saw the upturned hull of a large vessel in the area where the search had originated. Other bodies were picked up by the helicopter, and the Caister boat was instructed to take her sad cargo into Lowestoft harbour. Plans were made to take the *Shirley Jean Adye* back to Yarmouth, but just after they had set off they were directed back to Lowestoft to pick up some divers who would examine the hull of the sunken wreck to check that no-one was trapped inside. The weather was

The 'Shirley Jean Adye' prepares to launch.

"SKIPPER" JACK

"Skipper", second left, takes his place in the line-up of the Volunteer Rescue Service, 1987.

still too rough, however, and the search was again called off. The boat returned once more to Lowestoft harbour.

The year 1978 turned out to be a year of disaster for the Caister station. In December the lifeboat was called out to investigate flares, but as the boat was being launched a large wave overwhelmed her and the tractor. The boat was washed back on the beach and the tractor lost connection with the launching carriage, which ran into the sea below the low water mark. The gale swept sand over the carriage, and although its position was known it could not be recovered. The lifeboat, fortunately undamaged, was pulled back to the boathouse on skids, now stranded.

Many fruitless attempts were made to recover the carriage by Navy divers and local boats, but it remained firmly bedded in the soft sand. "Skipper" decided the time had come to ask a favour of his Dutch friends, and wrote describing the plight of the Caister service. It was then only a matter of time, and the right conditions, before the Dutch salvage company, Smit Tak International of Rotterdam, managed to recover it on June 15. These were the same people the Caister men had worked with back in 1955 at Waxham, and many old friendships were renewed. Restoration was needed, and this work was undertaken by the original builders of the carriage, Crane Fruehauf of Dereham. The lifeboat was eventually put back on the carriage on December 1, 1979, having been out of service for almost a year. Three days later it was launched, and rescued eleven men from a trawler.

Although never officially rewarded for his lifeboat services by the RNLI, "Skipper" was, in September, 1984, together with the other members of the lifeboat crew past and present, given the Freedom of the Borough of Great Yarmouth. At a unique ceremony held at the Town Hall the Caister men, together with the Gorleston lifeboatmen, were honoured by the town for their past services. The award to Caister was the first of its kind ever made to a privately run lifeboat station. Among the 100 past and present crew members from the two stations, the oldest was 95-year-old Charles Knights of Caister, whose father had been a lifeboatman from 1885 until 1941 and was a survivor of the 1901 *Beauchamp* disaster.

Although "Skipper" had made an appearance on local television back in the early 1960s, it is the programme made in 1987 that he remembers as one of the highlights of his life. An appeal had been launched earlier that year to raise £400,000 to buy a new lifeboat for the station, and the appeal committee looked at every method available to get their message across to the public. When the opportunity came for "Skipper" to appear on Terry Wogan's famed BBC "Wogan" show,

"Skipper" pictured on his 70th birthday.

Woodhouse and Wogan - 3rd April 1987. Terry Wogan admitted "he stole the show".(BBC Enterprises)

including a ten minute chat with Terry Wogan, it was an occasion not to be missed. A BBC chauffeured limousine arrived at Caister to take "Skipper," David and two other members of the crew to London where they were entertained before the show. Not put off when told he would have to be "made up," he told the make-up girl, "Oh yes, I'm used to all that stuff 'cause when we can't get off we do a Punch and Judy show on the beach."

Throughout the interview he entertained millions of viewers with his seafaring tales and unassuming manner, and took the opportunity to appeal for funds for the new lifeboat by telling everybody where to send their money. Following the programme Terry Wogan was quoted in the local Press as saying: "He was a terrific performer, wonderful old sea salt and natural talker. If I am shipwrecked off Caister I hope it is 'Skipper' who comes out to rescue me... so long as he learns to swim."

This last comment was a response to "Skipper's" revelation on the show that he could not swim. "Fishing families told their young to keep out of the water," he said with a wry smile.

Today, "Skipper" has to content himself with more shore based work, but on occasions still takes his place in the lifeboat crew. His experience makes him an invaluable member of the Rescue Service, his advice being sought on many problems, and particularly those mechanical. Lifeboat engines differ from the ordinary marine engine, as do the electrical systems, mainly due to the RNLI setting their own standards and using their own components. In a specialist field such as this there is no substitute for experience and this, with seven decades now behind him, is something "Skipper" has plenty of.

When the conditions are right he goes fishing and still maintains his own boats. A lot of time is taken up with helping the £400,000 appeal launched to buy a new purpose built lifeboat for Caister. Although no final decisions can be made as to what boat to buy, one of the options under consideration is a 38ft self-righting boat of a design at present used in a variety of commercial situations. This boat could be modified for carriage launching, and boats of the same design are at present used by the National Sea Rescue Service of South Africa, and in Bermuda.

As stated in the introduction to this book, "Skipper" is the custodian of many books and documents relating to the earlier days of the Caister beachmen, and now with more time to read and research he has become an authority on lifeboat history. He is often asked to speak on this at various functions and fund raising events. His talks on the lifeboat history, interspersed with his personal reminiscences, make facinating listening.

April 15, 1988, was also a milestone in "Skipper's" eventful life, for 86 years after his great-grandfather had been introduced to the King at Sandringham, "Skipper" was himself to meet a prominent member of the Royal family, His Royal Highness the Prince of Wales, not at a Royal

April 15th 1988 and "Skipper" is introduced to HRH The Prince of Wales during the royal visit to the Caister Station.(S L Tasker)

residence, but on his home ground, at the lifeboat station.

The Royal visit had been arranged as part of the "Keep the Boat Afloat" appeal, and in the weeks before the great day the crew and members of the appeals committee spent many hours preparing the boat and the station. "Skipper" and David Woodhouse had been involved from the very beginning, and as the prestigious day approached "Skipper" was among the people consulted by officials concerning the details and security of the visit. It was considered essential that the lifeboat shed should not be covered with flags or decorated specially for the occasion. The Prince was to see a working station, ready to launch at any time. Not one to get excited about things, "Skipper" took it all in his stride, his only concession being to buy himself a new cap. And that, he insisted, was because he needed a new one, anyway.

It was a typical east coast day, misty, with an easterly wind sweeping in from the sea, when His Royal Highness arrived accompanied by the Lord Lieutenant of Norfolk and the mayor of Great Yarmouth. After being introduced to the crew the Prince was shown over the lifeboat by the coxswain. Then the most memorable part of the day happened. The Prince was offered a trip out to sea in the boat, an offer which, although behind in his schedule, he had no hesitation in accepting - much to the delight of the watching crowds, but even more important, to the members of the volunteer service.

When the boat returned to shore it was "Skipper's" turn. The official programme continued: Councillor Weymouth (Chairman of the Appeal Committee) will ask leave to present: Mr Jack ("Skipper") Woodhouse, Veteran Crew Member.

When "Skipper" spoke to the Prince he discovered he already knew about the "Wogan" show, and a brief conversation followed about "Skipper's" involvement with the lifeboat since 1927. One nautical person to another.

This was followed by a presentation when crew member Paul Durrant gave the Prince a box of Caister kippers, specially caught and smoked for the occasion by the coxswain Benny Read.

This was the first time in the long history of the station that a member of the Royal family had paid a visit, and indeed, the first time Caister had seen such an event. Hundreds of local people and schoolchildren were on the beach and dunes. Earlier in the day, standing on his own in front of the shed, "Skipper" said he could not help remembering occasions from the past, such as the times during the war years when the soldiers stood guard outside the shed with fixed bayonets, and that unhappy day when the RNLI lifeboat was taken out for the last time. The shed had played such an important part in his life it had sometimes become a second home.

"Skipper" and his brother David will be the last in the Woodhouse line. Undoubtedly in the years to come there will be many more interesting incidents and characters to record, but the traditional beachman is a dying breed, and the beaches of the East Coast will not see any more "Skippers."